William Stoner
and the
Battle for the Inner Life

BOOKMARKED

STEVE ALMOND

PUBLISHING
NEW YORK, NY

Printed in the United States of America.
First Edition

Author's Note

This is a work of non-fiction. I've changed a few names. Memory is not transcription, of course, but I've done my best.

Ig Publishing
Box 2547
New York, NY 10163

www.igpub.com

ISBN: 978-1-63246-08-75

For my mother

A hero is one who wants to be himself."

—Ortega y Gassett

By Way of Introduction

Let Us Now Praise Unfamous Men

In the autumn of 1995, at the age of 28, I abandoned a career in journalism to pursue the dubious goal of writing short stories. My selection of a graduate program was eased considerably by the paucity of my talent. I applied to twenty schools, was admitted to three, and offered financial aid by one, a state university nestled in the polite and muggy suburbs of the south.

I rented a carriage house whose central allure was a gleaming antique bathtub that seemed to portend my future. I yearned to become the sort of writer who spent hours bleeding truth onto the page before collapsing into a scalding soak. Everyone in the program dreamed the same dream. If we worked hard enough, if we read the right books, if we charmed the prevailing mentors, our work would be plucked from the slush pile, gussied up for publication and bound into handsome volumes by the Bad Parents of New York City. At precisely this point, everyone who had ever rejected us would be forced to admit the terrible mistake they had made.

I was particularly inept at disguising my aims, and would eventually become so reviled that the fiction faculty barred me from attending workshops and refused to read my thesis. All that comes later. I mention these circumstances only to suggest my frame of mind when I first encountered *Stoner*.

This happened a few months into the program, at a party hosted by my friend Dan Belkin. We were getting to know one another with the help of some affable drugs when he asked if I'd ever read *Stoner*. I eventually discerned that he was referring to a novel, which I assumed would be a tale of hydroponic hi-jinx. It is not. The author, John Williams, begins:

> *William Stoner entered the University of Missouri as a freshman in the year 1910, at the age of nineteen. Eight years later, during the height of World War I, he received his Doctor of Philosophy degree and accepted an instructorship at the same university, where he taught until his death in 1956. He did not rise above the rank of assistant professor, and few students remembered him with any sharpness after they had taken his course.... Stoner's colleagues, who held him in no particular esteem when he was alive, speak of him rarely now; to the older ones, his name is a reminder of the end that awaits them all, and to the younger ones it is merely a sound which evokes no sense of the past and no identity with which they can associate themselves or their careers.*

*

To understand how audacious I found this opening, you would have to know how loyal I was, back then, to the dogma of the MFA program, the smothering exhortations to *show, don't tell*. Because I lacked confidence in the stories I was trying to write, because those stories were at best half-formed, I reliably plunged my readers into the consciousness of some poor schlub in the midst of an unspecified crisis. I assumed this chaos would beguile readers, that they would hunger for all the facts I withheld from them. I was writing almost entirely out of my insecurity, which explained the inflamed prose, the preposterous plot twists, and glib dialogue.

It wasn't just the flat expository style of *Stoner* that flummoxed me. Williams had opened his novel by drily announcing the insignificance of his protagonist. I assumed the point of literature was to document the lives of the driven and depraved, the lawless and lust-riven, in short: the memorable.

It hadn't occurred to me that the story of every life is, from a cosmic perspective, one of obscurity. You are alive for some brief span, then you die. The great mirage of human consciousness is that our striving deeds will render us immortal. It might be said that I had confused literature with history, which serves as the de facto press office of the infamous. This confusion redounded to my own ambitions. I wanted from literature to be known by the world. I had missed the point: Literature exists to help people know themselves.

None of this occurred to me on that first night. I remember only that I read *Stoner* in a spell, and that I wept a good deal, inexplicably though not unhappily.

*

The novel's central events can be summarized in a single sentence: Stoner, the only son of subsistence farmers, attends college, unexpectedly falls in love with literature, and becomes a teacher; he endures a disastrous marriage, a prolonged academic feud, and a doomed love affair, then falls ill and dies.

The book refuses to hurtle Stoner toward a traditional conception of heroism. He does not fight in a war or launch a doomed expedition. He does not ascend the ranks or vanquish his foes or risk all for love. He is often excruciatingly passive, constrained by the conventions of his age and the inhibitions of his character. *Stoner* enthralls precisely because it captures with unbearable fidelity the moments of internal tumult that mark every human life.

Sometimes these are moments of regret or guilt or disappointment. Just as often they are moments of ecstatic revelation. The first of these occurs his sophomore year in college, during a required survey of English literature. To this point, the course has bedeviled Stoner. He reads and rereads the assignments but can find no meaning in the words. Toward the end of one class, his professor, an imperious figure named Archer Sloane, reads Shakespeare's 73rd Sonnet and demands to know what Stoner makes of it.

The poem is genuinely bewildering. The basic idea, barely visible beneath a tangle of naturalistic metaphor and vexing pronouns, is that our apprehension of mortality should inspire us to cherish the world of our youth. Stoner sits, awkwardly wedged into his wooden desk. The professor reads the poem again, this time tenderly, "as if the words and sounds and rhythms had for a moment become himself."

Stoner can summon no words, but the world around him suddenly takes on a phantasmagoric intensity. Light slants from the windows and settles upon the faces of his fellow students. He watches one blink and notices as a thin shadow falls upon a cheek "whose down has caught the sunlight." Stoner marvels at the intricacy of his hands. He feels the blood flowing invisibly through his arteries. For several minutes after the others have left he sits dazed. He wanders the campus, taking in "the bare gnarled branches of the trees curled and twisted against the pale sky." He regards his fellow students curiously, "as if he had not seen them before, and felt very distant from them and very close to them."

The compression of sensual detail makes this passage read like a reverie, but something quite simple is happening: William Stoner is suddenly paying attention to his life.

*

It took me several years to absorb the essential lesson of *Stoner*, which is a precise repudiation of the idea I clung to back then. What matters is not the quality of a particular life, but the quality of attention paid to that life.

*

I didn't realize it at the time, but this was the reason I had fled journalism in the first place. As an investigative reporter, I was expected to document the escapades of notable scoundrels, dirty cops, con men, the whole sordid smorgasbord. My editors wanted an accretion of damning fact. But I kept pondering motive; what had possessed these people to self-destruct? "The interior life is a real life," as James Baldwin observes, "and the intangible dreams of people have a tangible effect on the world."

This line of inquiry did not sit well with my bosses. I can still remember the reaction offered by the owner of the newspaper chain for whom I worked. He had flown into town, as he did every year, to bawl us out for insufficient zeal. These reprimands usually happened at a fancy restaurant, where we could feel guilty for dining on his corporate credit card. When I announced my departure for grad school, he glared at me for a good half minute. "You want to write *books?*" he said finally.

I didn't know what to tell him. I just had a hunch I'd been investigating the wrong part of the human arrangement.

Stoner confirmed that hunch, more forcefully than any book I'd ever read. It exerts a stubborn grip on readers like me because it offers something increasingly rare in modern life: a dogged devotion to the inner life. By "inner life," I simply mean the private realm of thought and feeling through which we come to know ourselves. I stress the term because I believe our entire species is, at this perilous moment, engaged in a pitched battle for the inner life, one so pervasive it has become as invisible as air.

This struggle has been with us all along. It's ordained by consciousness. Among all creatures, humans face a unique burden. Do we choose to face the solitude of selfhood, the misfortunes engineered by fate and folly, the many ways we disfigure love into cruelty? But over the past half century (the course of my lifetime) this struggle has degenerated into an all-out assault.

To focus on the inner life today—to read books, to think deeply, to imagine with no ulterior agenda, to reflect on painful or confusing experiences—is to defy the clamoring edicts of our age, the buy messages, the ingrained habits of passive consumption and complaint. It is not yet a crime, merely an arcane and isolating practice.

There are obvious economic explanations. Vast sectors of our economy are devoted to the magical notion that potions and products and garish spectacle can banish our shame and doubt. And thus corporations, which promote and profit by a pervasive state of agitation, must eradicate the hauntings of the inner life.

The abrupt proliferation of technological devices has offered us the illusion of a mass confessional. But our phones and laptops more often represent a refuge from the tribulation of our internal experience. We turn to them in moments of anguish, rewiring our brains to seek diversionary stimulations. The frantic beckoning of our feeds has thus become another market for distraction, an array of "platforms" upon which we perform a market-ready version of our lives.

To read *Stoner* today is to recognize how shallow our conception of the heroic has grown. As a nation, we worship athletes and moguls and movie stars, those who possess the glittering gifts we equate with worth and happiness. Our realpolitik is dominated by a preening demagogue birthed in the oxymoronic swamp of reality television. The fictions that shriek across our screens are paeans to reckless ambition. This mania has infiltrated even our literary culture, with agents and editors stalking "larger than life" stories ripe for cross promotion.

It's not just that we're all toting around omniscient devices the size of candy bars. It's the staggering acceleration of our cognitive and emotional metabolisms: our hunger for sensation and narcissistic reward, our readiness to privilege action over contemplation. Our tireless compulsion to be known by the world rather than seeking to know ourselves.

Where does that leave a figure such as William Stoner, a timid medievalist who spends his life studying ancient manuscripts? Long before his retirement, he is regarded as a relic around campus. He would qualify as a fossil today.

*

William Stoner will dwell in obscurity forever. But that, too, is our destiny. Our most profound acts of virtue and villainy will be known only by those closest to us, and forgotten soon enough. Even our deepest feelings will lay concealed within the vault of our hearts. The reason we construct fame fantasies is to hide from these dire truths. By burnishing our public personae, we seek to escape the terror of facing our hidden selves. What marks *Stoner* as such a subversive work is that it portrays this confrontation not as a tragedy, but the essential source of our redemption.

Stoner knows his place in the world. He knows that others find him absurd, a footnote in the great human story. Over and over again, he is slammed up against his own inadequacies as a son and father and husband and scholar. And yet he refuses to turn away. As Stoner lies dying, a softness enfolds him, and a languor creeps upon his limbs. "A sense of his own identity came upon him with a sudden force, and he felt the power of it. He was himself, and he knew what he had been."

How many of us can say the same of ourselves?

*

In the years since my first fervid encounter with the novel, I've read *Stoner* a dozen times. I never quite mean to. I don't get up in the morning and think to myself, *Hey, why don't I read* Stoner *again*? I'll just be wandering around my office, frisking the shelves for inspiration; an hour later I'm forty pages in and beyond rescue. I've probably read more pages of the book standing up than sitting down.

What I want to argue in this peculiar pint-sized ode is that our favorite novels aren't just books. They are manuals for living. We surrender ourselves to them for the pleasures they provide, and for the lessons they impart.

I've learned more about craft from reading *Stoner* than any workshop I ever took, and spent years studying the technical intricacies that fortify its limpid prose. *Stoner* has also helped me find clarity amid the mass delusions of our age. In its own restrained manner, the novel casts a piercing light upon the worship of power and wealth that has corroded our national spirit.

But the central reason I keep circling back to *Stoner* isn't aesthetic or moral. Deep down, what I'm after is personal reckoning. Each time I've read the book, it has illuminated some new aspect of my own inner life, as I've evolved from student to teacher, from bachelor to husband and father, from a son in mourning to a man staring down his own mortality.

We cherish certain books precisely because they wield this power of intimate revelation. We read them to be enchanted, to be transported out of ourselves, but most centrally, to know ourselves more deeply. That process is no picnic. Reading *Stoner* has become an increasingly painful experience for me over the years—almost unbearable, as you'll see.

And yet I find tremendous hope in the fact that the novel has endured within an empire whose industrial energies are dedicated to annihilating the inner life. Like a medieval manuscript, it has been passed from one reader to the next, a fragile and exquisite reminder that a meaningful life arises from the willingness to pay attention, especially when it hurts to do so.

1. The Fall and Rise of Stoner

Because writers so often toil in obscurity, and because nearly all of them believe this obscurity to be unjustified, the tale of *Stoner's* resurrection has been invoked repeatedly as a literary article of faith. The saga affirms that petulant voice inside every writer, the one that insists publishing is ultimately a meritocracy, that posterity isn't about trends or marketing budgets or hype. Dickinson sent her miniature epics to friends who regarded them as little more than strange birds. Herman Melville figured *Moby Dick* would be his opus magnum and was shocked when it paved his descent into oblivion. *The Great Gatsby* was dismissed for years as a minor work. The beat goes on.

It's also important, and oddly inspiring, to recognize the shape John Williams was in when he wrote *Stoner*. As Charles Shields documents in his scrupulous new biography, T*he Man Who Wrote the Perfect Novel: John Williams, Stoner, and the Writing Life*, he was besieged on all fronts. Although he had two novels to his name, he was barely known within the literary firmament.

His first novel, *Nothing but the Night*, was put out by a tiny Denver imprint run whose publisher, Alan Swallow, would become his mentor. Williams moved to Denver to help Swallow run the press and to earn a PhD at the University of

Denver, where he wrote poetry and criticism. He soon came to regard his debut as an embarrassment.

His second novel, *Butcher's Crossing*, came out with a major publisher, Viking, in 1959. It tracks a young Harvard dropout who travels to the Kansas outback of the 1870s and embarks on a catastrophic buffalo hunt—Cormac McCarthy by way of Emerson. *The New York Times* dismissed it as a failed western that "contains little excitement and moves as though hauled by a snail through a pond of molasses." (It should be noted that the reviewer was the author of numerous pulp westerns who wrote under the pen name Clem Colt.)

By the time Williams sent off his third novel, his third marriage was imploding, his previous work was out of print, the Guggenheim Foundation had declined his application, and his poetry had been met with indifference. His agent was no more encouraging about the initial draft of *Stoner*. "I may be totally wrong," Marie Rodell wrote, "but I don't see this as a novel with high potential sale." Most of the editors who received the book concurred. One referred to Stoner as a "pale gray character."

*

There are any number of writers who might have capitulated in the face of so much bad data. Myself, for instance. Had I received such a prognosis from Rodell, I would have fired back a note along the lines of this:

Dear Marie,
Stoner is too dull, you say? That was my hunch too.

Fortunately, in previous drafts I had the professor stran-
gle his wife and bludgeon his academic rival with an
original folio of The Canterbury Tales. He also decapi-
tates a babysitter because she witnesses one of the killings.
Then he abducts his daughter and they set off on a crime
spree that carries them from Missouri to the Badlands of
South Dakota, where he meets a Native American sha-
man, whom Stoner murders and eats. Would that help?

Steve

Thrilled as I am to have initiated the very unpromising subgenre of *Stoner* Fan Fic, my point is this: Williams's faith never wavered. "Oh, I have no illusions that [*Stoner*] will be a 'best seller' or anything like that," he told his agent. "The only thing I'm sure of is that it's a good novel; in time it may even be thought of as a substantially good one."

As this note suggests, Williams was the temperamental opposite of his fictional creation: a confident artist who obsessed over his reputation. Shields describes how Williams would camp out in a conspicuous spot in the English department every time one of his novels came out and wait for his colleagues to congratulate him. They rarely did.

Envisioning this scene, I felt a twinge a pity for Williams. But *of course* he was needy. *Of course* he had a big ego. How else would he have withstood the setbacks he suffered? How else would he have converted into creative fuel the doubts the world inflicted on him?

*

These doubts did not end with the publication of *Stoner* in 1965. The book received a few kind notices, sold a couple of thousand copies, and sank from public view. One of the indignities Williams suffered was news that the novel written by his boorish brother-in-law and published a month before his own had sold twice as many copies. As Rodell predicted, *Stoner* proved woefully out of step with the sensibilities of American readers.

Except that phrases such as the preceding one are complete nonsense. There is no such thing as "the sensibilities of American readers." It's one of those terms invented by people in publishing so that they can pretend to have some inkling of what books will sell.

There are certainly brand name authors who can be counted upon to move units, and books that enjoy massive promotional support, and books that receive glowing reviews in major venues, and books written in response to particular cultural crises. There's no doubt, for example, that a work such as James Baldwin's story collection, *Going to Meet the Man*, was bound to receive attention in 1965, given that the nation's TV screens were awash in images of Alabama state troopers clubbing civil rights protestors. All of this helps in the short term.

But for a work of literature to endure, it has to induce a visceral emotional response in readers, the sort that convinces them other people *must* read the book. This sort of evangelism is essential because of the time and attention that novels demand. In this sense, *Stoner* enjoyed a massive advantage that nobody foresaw. Namely, that its concerns—the redemptive power of literature, pedagogic integrity, the academy as a refuge—appealed to the very people most likely to be passionate readers and influential critics.

*

I don't say this to take anything away from *Stoner*. Williams didn't write the book to pander to starry-eyed adjunct professors such as myself. It arose, organically, from his own preoccupations as student and teacher of literature. But it's also true, and not entirely coincidental, that Williams was a pioneer in the world of creative writing programs, which has expanded exponentially over the past few decades.

There are now a thousand such programs in America, all of them stocked with aspiring writers who struggle to convey the pleasures of reading to disinterested undergraduates, to produce original work, and to contend with rivalries, just as William Stoner did. Most every person who enrolls in these programs has, like Stoner, used literature to access his or her own inner life. The rise of MFA culture—so frequently assailed by self-appointed by commissars of creativity—amounts to a mass movement of people who have gone in search of themselves.

The absurdities of academia have inspired a raft of comedic novels (*Lucky Jim, White Noise, Moo, Straight Man*). But there is also a hunger for books that portray the dignity of the academy, and celebrate the life of the mind. Such earnest motives may sound outdated in a world overrun by the protective pleasures of irony and satire. It's also how a lot of us feel. *Stoner* is one of the few novels that honors our idealism.

*

To put it in rock and roll terms, *Stoner* became the Velvet Underground of novels. As Brian Eno quipped, only 10,000 people bought the band's debut album, but all of them started bands. Very few people knew *Stoner* existed when it was published. But a startling number were writers and critics, and virtually all of them became passionate advocates.

The charter member of the Cult of *Stoner* was Irving Howe, who cited the book just a year after its publication in *The New Republic*. "Given the quantity of fiction published in this country each year, it seems unavoidable that most novels should be ignored and that among these a few should nonetheless be works of distinction," Howe observed. "*Stoner*, a book that received very little notice upon its appearance several months ago, is, I think, such a work: serious, beautiful and affecting." By 1973, C.P. Snow opened his review of the British edition with the question every *Stonerian* has posed since: "Why isn't this book famous?"

One of the curiosities of this saga is that Williams himself had, a year earlier, won the National Book Award for *Augustus*, his fictional account of the life of the first Roman emperor. The American edition of *Stoner* went out of print anyway.

In 1981, the writer Dan Wakefield ran a long appreciation of Williams in *Ploughshares*, and worked tenaciously to convince another publisher to reprint *Stoner*. Eventually the director of the press at the University of Arkansas, Fayetteville—where Williams had come to spend his final years—agreed to reprint the novel. This reissued edition was out of print by the time it was pressed into my hands, a decade later.

The pattern repeated itself. Writers continued to pen paeans, specialty booksellers couldn't keep the novel in stock, and eventually one of them mentioned this oddity to the editor of the *New York Review of Books* imprint, which reissued the book in 2006. The literary historian Morris Dickstein reignited interest with a piece in the *Times* anointing *Stoner* "the perfect novel." Soon, prominent novelists from the UK such as Colum McCann, Ian McEwan, and Julian Barnes were trumpeting *Stoner*.

If the fate of *Stoner* in America amounted to a series of bonfires, in Europe the book ignited a wildfire, leaping from the bestseller list of one country to the next: Germany, France, the UK, Italy, the Netherlands. It is genuinely perplexing that the story of quiet professor living in Missouri in the middle of the twentieth century would electrify European readers. I can only speculate as to why.

Perhaps in smaller countries, passionate affiliation to a literary novel goes viral more easily. Perhaps European readers found in *Stoner* a thrilling departure from the American image most commonly exported overseas, that of men in pursuit of glory by means of restless mayhem. Perhaps they were beguiled by a hero who rejects war in favor of a monastic devotion to medieval manuscripts. Perhaps in the quiet dignity of William Stoner they found the flickering of an American enlightenment. Whatever the case, Europeans purchased more than a million copies.

*

I've recommended *Stoner* incessantly. Years ago, I foisted the book upon a young writer with whom I'd just read, though foisted doesn't quite capture the spirit of imploration involved. A month later, she wrote to confess that she had started reading *Stoner* but had put the book down, because she had gotten into a fight with her boyfriend and was in the midst of moving out and reading the book was more than she could bear. A second note arrived a few days later, informing me that she had finished *Stoner*. "It kind of wrecked me," she wrote. "But it also made me feel—this is a little hard to explain—that I needed to be wrecked."

At the first book group discussion of *Stoner* I ever led, a former colleague of mine from Boston College appeared unexpectedly. He was an elderly professor of literature whom I had imagined as indifferent to modern novels. He sat in silence until the very end of the evening, when, with a certain hesitant ceremony, he withdrew a faded newspaper clipping from the breast pocket of his sport coat. He told us that he had been one of the few critics to review *Stoner* when it was first published and had dismissed the novel as arid and unoriginal, a minor work. I remember him staring at the clipping in bewilderment, as it were bloody blade that had materialized in his hand. "I can't imagine what I was thinking," he said softly. "I suppose I was a young man, jealous of the achievement."

At another book group, this one large and lubricated by wine, a man stood to address the room, his cheeks a roaring red. "Why should I read about this loser?" he demanded. "He refuses to fight for his country. His marriage is a nightmare. He gets bullied around at work. He never *does* anything." An awkward pall descended over the room, one broken by a second man who observed, quietly but with no less emotion, that he felt he was reading about his own life, and that William Stoner might as well have been him.

Both men were saying this, I think. It is this feeling of implication—of the novel revealing us to ourselves—that causes readers to have such extreme reactions.

*

Here in America, the ultimate measure of cultural relevance is the Hollywood makeover. I am duty-bound to note that a team of filmmakers was, until recently, in the midst of transforming *Stoner* into a major motion picture. The project has stalled, owing to accusations of sexual harassment against one of the stars. But given that the book is beloved by a number of A-list stars–including Tom Hanks and Ethan Hawke— there is little doubt *Stoner* will become a major motion picture eventually.

Should it come to fruition, the film will be seen by tens of millions of Americans. If even a fraction seeks out the book, *Stoner* will become a big deal—inasmuch as a novel can be a big deal these days—and will have completed its sojourn from cult status to mainstream adulation. William Stoner, or a camera-ready facsimile thereof, will appear at the Oscars. William Stoner will have a publicity team and an after party and a swag bag.

If you're detecting some snark here, it's because much of what makes a book sacred is the simple fact that readers get to make the movie. Your imagination does the work of all that labor listed in the credits. You can talk about the movie afterward with other people. But you've seen a different movie in a different theater, where you sat, alone with yourself.

The right filmmaker would understand this. In fact, the right filmmaker did. His name is Vernon Lott. I met him a decade ago, when I was teaching at the University of Idaho, in Moscow. Vernon, who lived nearby, asked me to appear in a documentary he was making about bad writing, of which I am a frequent practitioner and staunch advocate. After the interview, he asked if I could recommend any books of good writing. Not only did I recommend *Stoner*, I told him he should make his next film about it.

You know what happened next. Vernon wrote to me a couple of years later to announce that he was indeed making a documentary about *Stoner*. I had my doubts as to whether this would happen, given that his IMDB page listed "janitor" under the other jobs category. But Vernon did eventually show up at my house with a cameraman to record my earnest raving.

The resulting film, *The Act of Becoming*, is an hour long. It consists of a dozen writers and critics and editors staring into a single camera and talking about *Stoner*, how they discovered the book, why it became important to them. There are long shots of the prose itself, and the occasional pulsing of electronic music. At the very end of the film, Lott shows each of his subjects in the moments before our filmed interviews begin. We sit there staring into the camera, fidgeting, looking away, smiling nervously and blinking, licking our lips. These excruciating portraits fill the screen for two full minutes. They convey, rather magically, the point that every human being, if we dare to watch closely, lives in the midst of tumult.

Vernon managed to make a film that captures the artistic triumph of *Stoner*, which is not just that we witness the life of William Stoner, but that we witness our own.

2. The Unrivaled Thrill of Unrelieved Narration

I want to return briefly to the initial impression of *Stoner* offered by the author's agent, Marie Rodell. I am doing so not because I have a secret desire to humiliate literary agents— on the contrary, my desire to humiliate literary agents is quite public at this point—but because her assessment of the novel is so spectacularly wrongheaded. She fretted that *Stoner* would never sell because "its technique of almost unrelieved narrative is out of fashion."

In fact, the novel's narrative style is precisely what makes it so gripping. To trace out what I mean requires a crash course in the art of narration. I'll begin at the beginning.

Human beings are a storytelling species. Stories are how we construct ourselves and pluck meaning from the rush of experience. For most of our history as a species, the work of storytelling was done around a campfire. Teller and audience shared the same words, the same mythology, the same customs and cosmology. The invention of written and then printed stories initiated a disjunction. Suddenly, stories were being crafted for readers from another culture and another time. This required writers to create an entity—the narrator— capable of serving as a guide to the world of the story.

The narrator sets out the basic dramatic context of the

story, the properties of the world in question, the relevant histories, natures, and motives of the characters. At times, the narrator offers broader insights into human nature, generally traceable to the author. When the story moves into scene, the narrator swoops into a more subjective mode, offering us the psychic and sensual experiences of particular characters.

The authors of the great novels of the eighteenth and nineteenth century granted their narrators powers that would seem audacious by modern standards. Consider Tolstoy's famous opening to *Anna Karenina*:

> *All happy families are alike; each unhappy family is unhappy in its own way.*
> *All was confusion in the Oblonsky's house. The wife had found out that the husband was having an affair with their former French governess, and had announced to the husband that she could not live in the same house with him...*

Why does Tolstoy open with that sweeping generalization? Why not start with the tumult in the Oblonsky house, which so elegantly prefigures Anna's fate? Because Tolstoy needed to establish a narrator who could offer universal insights, who was concerned, not just about adultery, but the elusive nature of happiness.

What marks literature as distinct from any other artistic genre is this relationship we have with the narrator. Readers want to know that someone candid and highly observant is running the show. They want to be in congress with a compelling intellect. Without a narrator, a story isn't being told, it's just being.

*

It's important to reiterate here that Rodell was absolutely right to call *Stoner's* narrative style "out of fashion." The tradition of strong, independent narrators—exemplified in the American tradition by Henry James—had been on the wane for decades by the time Williams came along.

Modernist writers, most prominently James Joyce, introduced a new style of prose that sought to convey the ornate fluctuations of the mind, the swirl of sensations and insights, urges and inhibitions, that came to be known as stream-of-consciousness. In novels such as *A Portrait of the Artist as a Young Man*, and later, *Ulysses*, the hero's perceptions became the central form of action.

At the other end of the spectrum was the objective style of narration championed by Hemingway. His central innovation as a stylist was to write short declarative sentences in which description implied emotion and psychology. The attentive reader came to understand that Nick Adams was a traumatized veteran by the way he set up camp. Action became perception. To Hemingway, among the first writers born into the age of motion pictures, the narrator isn't an intellect or a sensibility so much as a carefully trained movie camera.

I mention these two writers because they epitomize opposing narrative strategies, both of which are widely imitated and (I'm sorry to report) continue to desecrate student manuscripts. I should know; I've read thousands in the past two decades.

To survey a particularly vexing subset of these, let us

return to the dawn of the millennium, when I worked as an Adjunct Professor of Bitterness at various Boston area colleges. Back then, I continually encountered stories in which the hero was an unnamed man, often unshaven, who woke in a strange hotel or bar or dorm room with no idea where he was or why. Invariably, something traumatic had happened to him and *to her*, a mysterious female pronoun—presumably his beloved. Our hero didn't know exactly what had happened though, because, as would eventually emerge, he suffered from anterograde amnesia, a rare form of short-term memory loss that afflicts vast numbers of fictional characters. In an effort to remain loyal to the protagonist's disorientation, the remainder of the story consisted of frenetic scene fragments, chronologically mutilated for maximum profundity.

My standard reaction to these pieces was to jot earnestly flummoxed queries in the margins such as "Where are we?" and "Are the italics flashbacks?" and "Is it possible I'm missing a page?" Then office hours would roll around and I would say to the author, "I found your story really ambitious, Jason, but I'm not sure I totally understood it."

Jason would look at me with the sort of pity summonable only by a college sophomore and utter the six words I came to dread: "Have you seen the movie *Memento*?" No, I would say, I hadn't seen that one, and Jason would explain that his story was inspired by *Memento*. Then Jason would recite the plot of that film, in its entirety, while I sat quietly in my cubicle chair mulling suicide.

In an effort to broach the virtues of more traditional narration I sometimes mentioned *Emma* by Jane Austen, at which point Jason would inform me that he had never seen that movie. This was back in the dark ages of the Internet. No social media. No Wifi. Cell phones were still dumb. My students read books, when assigned to do so by well-meaning primitives such as myself. But mostly they watched movies and TV shows.

Their style of narration thus managed to fuse the cinematic opacity of Hemingway with the claustrophobic interiority of Joyce. They lodged the camera behind the eyes of their protagonists but failed to establish who those protagonists were, where they were, and what was at stake for them. The reader thus wound up in a state of unproductive bewilderment. I say *unproductive* because there are, of course, productive forms of bewilderment. We write stories precisely because we seek to make sense of the bewildering aspects of human endeavor: love, loss, desire, regret. These stories were more like language-based Sudoku puzzles.

*

Why do so many writers place the cart of action before the horse of narration? Often, we're simply driving blind. We don't know the story we want to tell when we sit down to write and hope action will lead us to the promised land of plot. Sometimes we know the world of the story so well that we forget the reader doesn't. But the most common culprit is insecurity.

The contemporary writer—steeped in the audio-visual pizzazz of screen-based storytelling—is likely to suffer an immediate and crushing sense of doubt. We feel that we must locate the impatient reader in a world so enveloping she will be unable to turn away. Thus, the dogma of show-don't-tell predominates, nurtured by workshops and later literary agents, who dismiss exposition as dull, mere info dumps.

We continually forget that readers don't want fancy prose. They want a narrator to tell them a story. In the absence of a narrator, the only way for a writer to deliver information is by having characters think or say it, which reduces characters to self-conscious and inefficient tools of narration.

Leaping into scenes without providing the necessary context requires writers to interrupt the action to insert this context, which forces readers to reinterpret what they've already read and blunts the forward momentum of the story. Too often, we use scenes to provide background information, mostly by having characters sit around thinking things. Not only is this pattern dull, it represents a misappropriation of scene.

Scenes are meant to instigate or escalate action, to isolate those instances when a character's destiny is disrupted by desire or misfortune or opportunity, when he is forced into conflict—with someone else and/or himself.

A few years back, I led a class examining the craft aspects of a single novel. To prepare, I evaluated every scene in *Stoner*, asking a simple question: what work does it do? I broke down a passage midway through the book, for instance, in which Stoner teaches a graduate seminar. This one unassuming scene *dramatizes* Stoner's talent as a teacher, his devotion to literature, his timidity in the face of conflict, the interplay between his passion and passivity, and his doomed idealism; it *introduces* two key characters, including his eventual love interest; and it *instigates* and *escalates* a budding rivalry. It does all this work simultaneously.

Storytelling is not some mystical pursuit. It is mostly about building psychologically and emotionally reliable ramps to moments that matter and then slowing down.

*

It was reading *Stoner*, over and over and over, that taught me these lessons. I wanted to understand, as a writer, the specific mechanisms of its enthrallment. The book begins with that blunt little obituary, which has the curious effect of shifting the reader's interest away from Stoner's achievements and toward an accounting of his internal experience.

What's less apparent about this opening, but just as crucial, is that it establishes a narrator capable of covering huge swaths of time and experience in a few sentences. This latitude allows Williams to present the precise moments that endanger his hero. Thus, barely two pages into the novel, Stoner's father proposes that his son go to college to study agriculture, a notion that has never occurred to the boy.

William, who has never been further than fifteen miles from home, has to swallow to steady his voice. Then he looks to his mother for counsel. What follows is a couplet that quivers with unspoken anxieties and regrets.

> *She said tonelessly, "You do what your pa says."*
> *"You really want me to go?" he asked, as if he half hoped for a denial. "You really want me to?"*

Williams reaches this crossroad so quickly because he relies on vivid exposition to convey the grinding routine and grim prospects of farm life. Rather than dragging the reader through lengthy scenes of Stoner toiling in the fields, slopping the pigs, and casting wistful gazes at the horizon, we get only the scene that matters, as Stoner struggles to reckon with the upheaval of his life.

Two hundred words later, our hero has reached the university, where he feels an unprecedented serenity. A few pages after that, Archer Sloane reads a Shakespeare sonnet and Stoner's world explodes again. He settles on becoming a teacher, but hides this decision from his parents. No sooner has he confessed to them when World War I begins, and he has to decide whether to enlist. Then he falls in love with Edith and marries her, and must immediately confront that the union is a disaster.

Every few pages Stoner is slammed up against some harrowing realization, some impossible decision, some uncontrollable urge. There is no down time. This relentless pacing is a direct result of the narration Rodell disparaged as *unrelieved* and *out of fashion*. But Williams understood what he was up to. "A great deal more is going on in the novel than appears on the surface," he assured his agent, "and its technique is a great deal more 'revolutionary' than it appears to be."

What he meant, I think, is that he had hit upon a strategy that combined objective efficiency and subjective intensity in pursuit of one man's inner life. Most novels, after all, marshal their energies toward the fulfillment of a particular goal: a marriage must be made, a love consummated, a crime punished, a sinner redeemed, a feud settled, a family repaired. William Stoner fulfills several of these goals. But *Stoner's* attention remains fixed not on public outcome but private reverberation.

Of Williams's contemporaries, the only novelist I can think of who attempts something similar is Evan S. Connell (*Mrs. Bridge and Mrs. Bridge*). This is not to suggest that John Updike and Saul Bellow and Tony Morrison don't offer us deep access to the consciousness of their characters. But these novelists—among the most influential of their age—allot their energies to broader goals: explorations of race, cultural morality, and philosophical inquiry. Most of their books have elaborate plots and ensemble casts and what the critics dependably refer to as "an indelible prose style."

In *Stoner*, Williams sought to perfect what he called "the plain style," an approach he traced back to Stoicism, which emphasized reason over emotion, and sentences whose power derived from naturalistic description rather than stylistic flourishes. When Williams speaks about the novel as revolutionary, I take him to mean that he created a narrator at once omniscient and transparent, able to depict his hero with an unvarnished precision *and to* fathom the deepest regions of his psyche, a narrator that wed the virtues of Hemingway and Joyce.

*

There are other notable aspects of *Stoner* that contribute to its potency. For instance, the novel is entirely devoid of subplots. Every expository passage presages a scene in which Stoner is forced to act, and every action he takes drives the story forward. The plot turns not on coincidences but confrontations that register as astonishing and inevitable.

Williams also limits his supporting cast, all of whom play

complex and shifting roles in Stoner's life. Edith begins as an object of desire, becomes his chief antagonist, and winds up a loyal companion. Hollis Lomax is a potential friend before he curdles into a bitter rival.

One of the central challenges of this approach is that Stoner himself, while learned, is not a deeply reflective person. He has intense emotional reactions to the world, and a steadfast conscience, but he is often blind to his own motives and intentions. This is a challenge for any novel, especially one so narrowly focused on a single character's experience.

Novelists in the tradition of Thackeray and Austen and George Eliot met this challenge by allowing their narrators to editorialize, to batter their benighted characters. Williams does not. His narrator remains an impartial (if ruthless) observer, not a commentator.

Instead, he surrounds Stoner with characters who assail him with the truths he cannot or will not see. Chief among these is Archer Sloane, the man who identifies Stoner's calling as a teacher. Just as significant is Dave Masters, one of two friends Stoner makes as a graduate student, who exposes Stoner's grandiose delusions about academia. Both men haunt Stoner. They are the dark prophets who illuminate his destiny.

*

What's most inspiring about the writing of *Stoner* is that John Williams began his career writing in precisely the same manner as those undergraduates who used to show up at my office hours to discuss their *Momento* rip-offs. I know this because some years ago a fellow Stonerian sent me a copy of Williams' appalling debut novel, *Nothing But the Night*, which opens like this:

> *In this dream where he was weightless and unalive, where he was a pervading mist of consciousness that seethed and trembled in a vast stretch of dark, there was at first no feeling, only a dim sort of apperception, eyeless, brainless, and remote, whose singular ability was to differentiate between himself and the darkness.*

I am sorry to report that this ectoplasmic drivel continues for several more pages. We are trapped inside the addled mind of some unidentified male who can barely make out his surroundings. It's actually more garishly inchoate than any student work I've ever received. Here's how the first chapter *ends*:

> *Subtly, easily, soundlessly, as if he were an intangible atmosphere, he merged with the resting body, became one with it in a sudden and inexplicable chemistry, realized in a brief flash of agony that this was his real identity, that this was himself; and just before the curtain of dark fell, he looked up out of the young man's abruptly opened eyes, saw the needless sea of the crowd's face, heard again the animal scream of its hatred, felt their brutal hands upon his body, saw their fists upraised to smash bloodily downward, felt an instant shock of pain, and then the sea of blood darkened and he swam in utter blackness and knew no more.*

To reiterate: this prose was crafted by the same person

who wrote *Stoner*.

Alan Swallow, who published *Nothing But the Night*, was refreshingly blunt about its faults. It lacked "a certain consistency or observable direction of development" and indulged in "rather deliberate obscurantism." Swallow believed his protégé might be the sort of writer "who needs to throw away two or three novels before the thing starts clicking."

Williams was too headstrong to throw away his novels. But he learned from their mistakes. His second book managed to bleed out the calculated confusion and overwrought prose. But the story revealed a writer still driven to court the epic, one who relied on vivid landscapes and bloody action to compensate for a lack of character development.

That Williams eventually wrote *Stoner* into being attests to the author's imagination and native talent, but more so to his humility. It took him two decades, but he managed to eradicate his impulse to impress the reader. His third novel represents a sustained and monumental act of attention. Take it as a radical, even revolutionary, example of what happens when writers silence their egos, ignore the fraudulent wisdom of the marketplace, and place their faith in the virtues of unrelieved narration.

3. Love Makes Us Zombies (aka Worst Marriage Ever)

The list of literary characters undone by marriage is long and illustrious. Listen to Madame Bovary hold forth. "Each smile hid a yawn of boredom," she confides, "each joy a curse, each pleasure its own disgust; and the sweetest kisses only left on one's lips a hopeless longing for a higher ecstasy." Emma chases her longing through adultery and into suicide. This is to say nothing of the tribulations of the Archers (Isabel and Leland), the miserable Maples, the murderous Medea, the ill-fated Frank and April Wheeler.

The union of William and Edith Stoner appears relatively placid by comparison. And yet I can think of no other fictional pairing so devoid of affection, so animated by cruelty and manipulation. Their wreck of a marriage ranks as one of the novel's central pleasures.

This may sound perverse, unless you yourself have been married, in which case you know that such relationships—even as they provide love and companionship—can induce two otherwise reasonable people to discover the monstrous within themselves.

For most of human history, of course, marriage had little to do with joy or fulfillment. It was (and still is in many precincts) an economic institution designed to fulfill obligations not desires. Marriage shores up alliances, produces children for labor or inheritance, provides women a dubious measure of security and men a domestic kingdom to rule. Only in the last century or so, in the developed world, has the notion of marriage as a form of romantic destiny migrated from the world of fairytales.

Stoner suggests something darker than any other novel I've read, which is that the liberty to choose our betrothed is the ultimate booby trap, that our unconscious wishes direct us toward lovers guaranteed to afflict us, that we will ignore any and all warning signs along the way, will twist ourselves into knots to keep the peace, and ultimately choose a doomed loyalty over the pleasures of liberation. Pretty sick, huh?

*

William Stoner is twenty-eight years old, a newly minted professor of English nervously milling an academic reception, when he spots an elegant young woman pouring tea in the next room.

"Stoner paused in the doorway," Williams writes, "caught by his vision of the young woman." Note the construction of this sentence. Stoner doesn't notice a young woman. He is *caught by his vision* of her, as in trapped, ensnared, seized. And not by her. By his vision of her, which is something else entirely. Desire immobilizes him for several moments, after which he backs out of the room in confusion. He cannot bring himself to look at her, though he thinks he can feel "the gaze of the young woman brush warmly across his face."

Stoner spots the host of the party and demands an introduction. The host is taken aback, along with the reader. To this point in the novel, we have seen no indication that Stoner harbors even a flicker of romantic want.

Edith Bostwick, he discovers, is twenty years old, the only child of a rich couple from St. Louis. She plays piano and has artistic inclinations fostered by her mother and plans to tour Europe in the spring. Stoner has no memory of learning these things. Their initial meeting is "blurred and formal" like the figured tapestry that hangs on a nearby wall. He is certain only of his own intentions; before Edith can leave the party, Stoner asks to call on her the next evening.

Edith opens the door and stands for several moments, as if she has not heard him. Cold air washes over Stoner's hot face. Finally, she turns and looks at him and blinks several times. She agrees to let him call, but does not smile.

*

Stoner shows up the next night at the home of Edith's aunt for an exceedingly awkward visit. At the end of the evening, Stoner asks to see her again. When she says nothing, he turns to go. At precisely this moment, Edith begins to speak in a "high shrill voice without inflection," recounting the details of her childhood. She doesn't appear to be talking to Stoner, though. Her eyes are fixed straight before her, as if she's reciting from "an invisible book."

Stoner wants to comfort her, to touch her even, but he remains paralyzed by puzzlement. He learns more about her from this abrupt soliloquy than he ever will again. "And when it was over," Williams writes, "he felt they were strangers in a way he had not thought they would be, and he knew that he was in love."

If this observation strikes you as somewhat askew, perhaps even bonkers, it is because romantic courtship generally involves the rapacious pursuit of intimacy, the desire to barge through the boundaries of selfhood, to imagine that we have known our beloved forever, which is to say: the opposite of a stranger.

Stoner and Edith are painfully shy, unversed in emotional discourse, and constrained by custom. But the behaviors they exhibit throughout courtship go beyond inhibition. They behave like zombies. I mean this literally. They address one another, but never seem to be in conversation. They march through dates as if programmed. Edith barely looks at Stoner. He reacts to her indifference and obvious psychic instability in the same manner a bull reacts to the matador's cape. Before she can depart for her planned tour of Europe, mere weeks after their meeting, Stoner proposes. Edith feigns shock.

"You must have known I loved you," Stoner declares.

"I didn't," she replies. "I don't know anything about that."

She's telling him the truth. But he won't hear it.

And so they stagger on. He meets her parents, who humiliate him for a few hours before offering a contemptuous blessing. The wedding is not an emotional event so much as a series of required actions, none of them remotely romantic, not even the marital buss ("her lips were as dry as his own"). Some of this disassociation is surely panic, the overloaded systems of two people unprepared for the commitment they are making to one another.

But that doesn't explain the fact that Edith ghosts Stoner at their reception, choosing instead to huddle with her family, who behave as if the occasion is a funeral—the death of the family's good name. When the groom catches sight of his bride across the room, he sees "a mask, expressionless and white." Not until they're on the train headed to St. Louis for the honeymoon does Stoner realize that it's all over, and that he has a wife.

*

The description of this honeymoon spans six excruciating pages. We know from the jump that Stoner's abject desire will be met by dread, because the narrator tells us so. And yet these scenes are among the most heart-rending of the entire book, because Williams does just what most writers lack the courage to do: he slows down where his characters are the most exposed and helpless.

Both newlyweds are virginal and inexperienced. But Stoner, who grew up on a farm, views the natural processes of life as unremarkable. Edith, by contrast, finds them "profoundly mysterious and unexpected. She knew nothing of them, and there was something within her which did not wish to know of them." The groom thus spends his wedding night obediently contorted on the sofa.

The next night, they share some champagne. Stoner walks up behind his wife and places his hands on her shoulders. She stiffens beneath his touch, her neck rigid, "the cords vibrant in their tensity." He urges her toward the bedroom and feels the resistance of her body and the "willed putting away" of this resistance.

Edith understands that she will be required to consummate the marriage. At this point, a lesser writer would hit fast forward to the act itself. Williams describes the bruising ballet that precedes the act, forcing us to witness the psychological and emotional violence of the encounter.

Stoner is dispatched to the bathroom by his bride. He emerges to find Edith in bed, the covers pulled to her chin, eyes closed, a thin frown creasing her forehead. She answers his entreaties with silence, and so he lays alone with his desire. Williams continues: "He moved his hand upon her; she did not stir; her frown deepened. Again he spoke, saying her name to silence; then he moved his body upon her, gentle in his clumsiness. When he touched the softness of her thighs she turned her head sharply away and lifted her arm to cover her eyes. She made no sound." Note the rhythm of the sentences here, the discrete precision of each independent clauses. Williams deploys syntax and grammar as emotional tools.

Afterwards, Stoner speaks to his wife affectionately. She responds by fleeing to the bathroom. He sees a light go on and hears her retch "loudly and agonizingly."

*

What's most ominous in all this is the simple fact that the Stoners have no way to communicate with one another. He recognizes his marriage as a failure within a month, and stops hoping it will improve soon after. "If he spoke to her or touched her in tenderness, she turned away from him within herself and became wordless." Silence becomes the default setting of their marriage.

Stoner knows his wife is unhappy, but lacks the courage to address her unhappiness. He takes her on picnics and buys her gifts. She merely withdraws further. They continue to have relations, an act Stoner completes as quickly as he can, while Edith buries her face in a pillow. Occasionally, she's drowsy enough that he can pretend her acquiescence is consent. When Edith does express emotion, it is in a veiled and hysterical manner. At their inaugural dinner party, she drinks too much and has a breakdown, berating Stoner and the other guests.

This is all happening in 1928, in a world of repressed, middle-class respectability. Divorce is never mentioned. Nor mental health. Instead, Edith decides—without warning—that she wants a child.

Her approach to the copulative events that this ambition requires can only be described as succubal. When Stoner returns from work one evening, he finds Edith lying naked on the bed, issuing odd little sounds. As Stoner approaches in alarm, these sounds become louder and her hands reach for him "like claws" tearing at his clothing. "Her mouth came up to him, gaping and hot … and all the time her eyes were wide and staring and untroubled, as if they belonged to somebody else and saw nothing." Edith's behavior isn't just animalistic, it's depersonalized; for the next two months she becomes a sex zombie. The moment she conceives, her carnal abandon pivots to disgust. Stoner, too, comes to regard this era of feral passion "as if it were a dream that had nothing to do with either of them."

Edith takes to her bed during her pregnancy, and becomes

a full-time invalid after the birth of her daughter, Grace, saddling Stoner with all domestic and parental duties. She wants nothing to do with the baby and demands that her husband buy her a house so she doesn't have to smell the soiled diapers.

By now, the fever of his desire has broken for good. Stoner is content to stay out of Edith's way, and to bond with his daughter. He even sets up at a tiny desk for her in his study. One evening, the two of them are in his office. Stoner makes a whimsical comment and the two of them begin to laugh. At precisely this moment, the door swings open and Edith stands outlined in the "hard light" from the next room. She announces that Stoner is trying to work and orders Grace out of the room.

"Don't you realize how unhappy she's been?" Edith snaps. She's confessing to her own sadness here, of course. But as anybody who has been married can tell you, projection is the last refuge of the cornered spouse. Edith knows Stoner and Grace have found refuge in each other—refuge from her—and she goes for the jugular:

> After her abrupt and almost brutal entrance into his study that night, an entrance which in retrospect seemed to him a surprise attack, Edith's strategy became more indirect, more quiet and contained. It was a strategy that disguised itself as love and concern, and thus one against which he was helpless.

Edith portrays her abduction as a product of Stoner's negligence, telling a visitor that Grace adores her father, but that he has no time for her. As Stoner overhears this declaration, his hands begin to shake. He confronts his wife, demanding that she stop using the child to punish him. Edith calmly calls his bluff. "All you could do is leave me, and you'd never do that. We both know it." When he returns from work that evening, Stoner discovers that Edith has removed all of his belongings from his study and piled them in a corner of the living room. She informs him that she will now be using his study as an art studio.

*

The Stoner marriage often plays as the drama of a pathological woman acting out, a situation I'll explore in the next chapter. But Williams also captures the quiet moments when one partner must confront the loss of esteem that undoes marriage. One evening, Stoner arrives home to find Edith asleep, her body "lax and wanton in its naked sprawl" and aglow like "pale gold." Her mouth, slightly opened, appears to be issuing cries of passion. He gazes at his wife for a long time, passing through a range of emotions that ends with "a weary sadness, for he knew that no longer could the sight of her bring upon him the agony of desire that he had once known."

What Williams is able to dramatize here, in a manner rarely achieved, is the profound confusion of marriage, the way we must bear so many conflicted feelings toward the same person. This is a moment of mourning for Stoner, the twilight of his passion; he no longer loves his wife in the way he once did. But alongside that revelation live other feelings—*distant pity, reluctant friendship, familiar respect*—which he cannot disavow.

The Stoner marriage is haunting, too, because it dramatizes a kind of isolation particular to modern matrimony. I don't want to idealize marriage in earlier eras, because it was most often a license for patriarchal abuse. But I do think that marriage used to take place within a much more cohesive familial and cultural framework. Couples could count on receiving support from kin, friends, and usually a religious community. The gender roles were far more constrictive. But there were a lot of people around to relieve the pressures on the bride and groom.

The Stoners have none of this. They live on what my wife and I sometimes call "the island of marriage." Because of their own particular histories, they cannot rely on their families for emotional or domestic support. Stoner has exactly one friend in the world, in whom he cannot confide. Edith has no one. They have to be everything to one another, though they have nothing in common, no way of understanding each other, and no basis of trust upon which they might build a true intimacy.

This is why Williams portrays them as zombies, I think: to suggest that they have no conscious capacity to choose one another. Stoner is dumbstruck at the sight of Edith and decides that he must marry her. She accedes to his ardor. They operate at the level of glandular instinct and social programming.

*

It's an extreme portrait, but anyone who has been in a long-term monogamy, especially a marriage, will recognize the outlines. Romantic love always begins with a dream, one designed to liberate us from the burdens of the past but inexorably bound to them. Erin and I dreamed of building a family impervious to the bullying and anxiety we'd experienced growing up, though our relationship was fraught with elements of both.

I've often portrayed our romance as a tale of heroic self-determination, in which we boldly hurtled from long-distance lovers to rookie parents in a few exuberant months. But I was consistently controlling during our courtship, and Erin too often silenced her doubts and resentments, for fear I would abandon her. Like William Stoner, I fell in love with an idea and charged ahead, ignoring the woman I claimed to adore.

Let us take as Exhibit A my insistence that we elope. Erin flew out for a long weekend. We snagged a vintage dress from a thrift store and made the two-minute drive to Somerville City Hall. Our honeymoon consisted of a couple's massage and takeout Indian. We were a couple of rebels who'd sidestepped family hassles and stuck it to the wedding industry; that was how I saw it. But to Erin, our DIY ceremony fit into a larger and more degrading pattern, in which I treated our love as something to be minimized, even concealed, rather than celebrated.

And the truth is, I remember almost nothing of the event itself, not the vows we uttered, nor the kiss, nor the emotions I felt. What I do remember—that my bride was besieged by morning sickness, that one of our two witnesses had a broken leg—speaks not to the glory of consummation but to the sense of injury around the event.

*

A dozen years into our marriage, I'm pleased to report that Erin and I remain happily betrothed. Even as we contend with three rambunctious kids, we're learning how to support one another as artists and parents. We laugh a lot. Our unofficial motto, invoked during moments of peak exasperation, is *No one gets out of this marriage alive!* Which speaks to a genuine desire that we will grow old together.

But our harmony has been hard won. The pain I inflicted on Erin during our courtship never went away. Nor did the mistrust and inhibitions bred into us by our families. We carried all that baggage with us over the threshold. And our marriage—like every marriage—has unpacked that baggage and hurled it around the room.

Without meaning to, Erin and I have reopened wounds inflicted long before we met. We've fought and frozen each other out. We've stormed out of restaurants and slept on couches. We've felt entrapped and typecast, and, in our worst moments, crushingly alone. This is why a significant and carefully silent part of myself feels actual relief when friends confide their marital woes. It's petty and despicable, especially the part where I return home and talk to Erin, pretending at grave concern when what I feel is a kind of brittle superiority.

We may not be rivals on par with Edith and William Stoner, but Erin and I (like all spouses) compete for time and space and regard. We withhold love when we feel deprived. We depend on each other and rage against our dependence. We expose the worst of ourselves and must therefore contend with shame on top of our disappointment.

I say this as someone who once smashed a bowl to bits on the floor of our kitchen, terrifying Erin, our two-year-old daughter, and myself. At vile moments such as this, I am no longer in control of my words or thoughts, no longer acting and reacting in the present. The neediness for love, the masculine doubt, the murderous aggression—it all takes over. I become a zombie.

This is why I cling to *Stoner* as such a powerful cautionary tale. It's not just about a brutally unhappy marriage. It's about the brutal ways in which marriage reveals all of us. And it's about what happens when a couple lacks the capacity to communicate and evolve. All that's left is the hurt. Erin and I have not stopped hurting one another. But we've developed a common language of trust, one that allows us (more often than not) to speak the truth without shame. We're learning to reflect and apologize. Day by day, we're unzombiefying our love.

4. Edith Stoner Is a Person, Not a Problem

In the spirit of full disclosure, I should note that Erin is herself a novelist. She's read and admires *Stoner*. But every time I mention the book (which is a lot) she offers the same observation: "There's a great novel to be written from the point of view of Edith Stoner." This is her diplomatic way of expressing what most women feel about *Stoner*, which is that it is, in its own quiet way, a deeply sexist book.

There's no doubt that Edith Stoner deserves her own novel, with all the privileges of understanding that a female-centered telling might provide (think *The Wide Sargasso Sea* by Jean Rhys). Nor is there any doubt that her rendering fits snugly within a tradition of female hysterics and vindictive schemers that dates back to Medea and Clytemnestra, Lady Macbeth and Ophelia, Bertha Rochester and good old Mrs. Havisham.

I happen to be writing in the midst of the furor over the Supreme Court nomination of Bret Kavanaugh, a man whose history includes multiple allegations of excessive drinking and sexually humiliating women. I mention him because the Senate hearing at which he and one of his accusers, Dr. Christine Blasey Ford, testified was such a dismal reminder that most stories in our culture center on the fury of wounded men. The magnetism of such figures has infiltrated our literature, our popular mythology, even the ostensibly somber task of vetting a judge for our highest court. This is why the media narrative that emerged from the hearing focused on the sneering, tear-stained rant of a judicial frat boy and his rage-drunk Senate wingmen, not the wrenching testimony of a woman Kavanaugh plainly assaulted.

This is the culture unleashed by the election of 2016, a culture sowed not just by whitelash, but its less celebrated corollary, dicklash. Consider the battle cry that unified the Republican National Convention, "Lock her up!" which has since become a Pavlovian response among those constituents whose broader mission is to criminalize female volition and ambition. Male rage doesn't just erase female trauma. It runs our country.

I am making this unpleasant excursion into the realpolitik because it has everything to do with Edith Stoner, and why she's become an even more problematic character over the years.

In so doing, I want to step briefly outside the domain of the novel to discuss the author himself. This is germane because *Stoner* is clearly his most autobiographical novel. In fact, Williams crafted a hero who represents an idealized version of himself. Stoner is humble, devout, principled, self-sacrificing, and (above all) blameless.

Williams shared some of these virtues. He was a devoted teacher and scholar. But by all accounts, most notably the new Shields biography, he was also a solipsist. He drank too much, conducted affairs, and put creative work before family. In short, he behaved with the impunity characteristic of the straight white male writers who came of age after World War II. His professional life was spent in the predominantly masculine preserves of academia. The women in his life served as support staff. Their job was to admire, encourage, and tend to the kids. Not surprisingly, men hold all the power in his novels.

Edith Stoner is the glaring outlier. And it's clear from the archival record that Williams struggled to bring her to the page. His agent, Marie Rodell, immediately flagged her portrayal as troubling. In the cover letter sent to one editor, she carefully noted, "This is not a final draft; John wants to do more with the wife's motivations." Rodell was no feminist; she had resigned as Betty Friedan's agent after reading *The Feminine Mystique* in manuscript.

*

Williams did labor to provide a deeper understanding of Edith. He pauses, in the midst of Stoner's headlong courtship, to fill in her backstory. We learn that Edith grew up in a formal and loveless home, her father vain and distant, her mother embittered and smothering. An awkward adolescence, during which she grew a foot in a single year—reaching a height "near that of a grown man"—intensifies her natural shyness. "Her moral training both at the schools she attended and at home, was negative in nature, prohibitive in intent, and almost entirely sexual."

But Williams clearly felt he had to do more to explain the extremity of her subsequent behaviors. Thus, midway through the book, we depart from Stoner's perspective for the first and only time, to follow Edith home after her father's suicide. It's an unnerving trip.

At the funeral, Edith is "curiously unmoved." As her father's casket descends, she lowers her face into her hands for several minutes—but her face is *expressionless*. After the burial, she spends several days in her childhood room. Callers assume she is secluded in grief, and her mother assures them that Edith and her father were "much closer than they seemed."

Edith is not grieving. She walks about the room "as if for the first time, freely." She sifts through her childhood possessions, "fondling them, turning them this way and that," then sorts them into two piles. Anything directly or indirectly related to her father she destroys. She burns the letters and clothes and pictures and even the stuffing from her dolls. Then she pounds the clay and porcelain heads of these dolls "to a fine powder" and sweeps the remains into a pile, which she flushes down the toilet.

It doesn't take a psychoanalyst to infer what Williams is getting at with all this, that Edith's father sexually abused her in some manner, and that this unprocessed trauma triggers the fanatical antagonism we see her exhibit toward her husband and daughter. She embodies an odd inversion of the standard patriarchal formula: female rage erases female trauma.

That's the math. And while some part of me admires the lucidity with which Williams dramatizes the psychological aftershocks of such trauma, another part of me can see the author straining to justify his portrayal of Edith as a monstrous hysteric.

Ultimately, this revelation underscores the novel's

masculine bias. Its basic message is that the world is seeded with abused woman and if you unwittingly woo one she will afflict you for the rest of your life. We are back in familiar province of Bertha Rochester and Miss Havisham, where female "madness" is not worthy of literary exploration, but serves instead as an obstacle to male fulfillment.

*

And that's if you *accept* my reading of Edith as the victim of abuse. Lots of readers don't. To them, she is merely as a contrivance, a cardboard villainess whose central narrative purpose is to burnish her husband's virtues. I can't argue with this interpretation. The physical descriptions of Edith render her more puppet than person. Her carriage is so stiff as to make her "every movement seem reluctant and grudging." The sharp bones of her face stretch her pale skin "as upon a framework" and her makeup is so thick that she appears to compose her features daily "upon a blank mask."

Williams infantilizes Edith. Her tantrums, her irrational projections, and her anarchic sexuality register as the behaviors of the very young. Like a toddler, she has only two modes: tyrannical and trivial. She either tortures her kin or pokes at clay. Because Edith displays no adult sense of volition, she is to be pitied rather than reviled.

But there is another possible portrait of Edith Stoner, one faintly visible beneath the author's energetically chauvinistic brushwork. What if Edith Stoner's rage is justified? What if her behavior is, in part, a rebellion against a life of marital and domestic entrapment? If the reader were allowed to consider the courtship from Edith's perspective, for instance, it would be hard to conclude that she actually *wants* Stoner's romantic attention. In fact, Stoner decides he loves Edith, not based on the content of her character but some set of romantic notions cribbed from literature. He then pursues her relentlessly, with almost no consideration of how she might feel.

Lost in all of this is the possibility that Edith might want some say in her own destiny, to choose a suitor she desires, or even to choose a life that doesn't involve suitors at all. Williams acknowledges Stoner as an intruder upon Edith's privacy. But based on their interactions, the courtship itself is the unwanted intrusion. Her muted reactions to his advances are not the result of ambivalence or even neurotic cogitation, but forced obedience.

Even if you don't believe Edith was molested by her father, it's possible to recognize her odd behaviors—shunning Stoner at the wedding, throwing up after their first copulative act—as arising from the simple fact that she doesn't love or desire the man who has insisted on becoming her husband. Haven't most brides, across the ages, felt as Edith does? The difference is that she refuses to quietly bend to the patriarchal yoke.

*

I'm not trying to defend Edith's hostilities. But I am suggesting that her conduct can be seen as an attempt to defend her sovereignty. The novel casts her artistic efforts as absurd. Her role is to sweep the hearth so that her husband can do meaningful work in the world. When she rejects this role, she is reduced from a person to a problem.

Here again, it's useful to remember the author's attitudes about gender. Williams sought out women who pledged allegiance to him, and his goals. He moved from one marriage to the next, often with intervening affairs, entirely preoccupied by his status among the other men within his academic and literary circles. In Edith Stoner, he created a woman powerful enough to repudiate this arrangement, to defy her husband, to relegate him to housework, to impose her own sexual agenda. Edith doesn't defer; she dominates. She doesn't nurture; she destroys.

Although I don't think this would have occurred to Williams consciously, his damning portrayal of her amounts to a punishment.

Such is the fate of female gender rebels in literature. Male authors inevitably transmute feminine rage at male oppression into a frenzied wrath that threatens everyone, innocents included. Call it the Lesson of Medea. Spurned by a cheating husband, she slaughters her romantic rival then her own children.

The effort to render Edith more plausible, in other words, didn't involve scaling back the scope of her cruelty, or (more ambitiously) plumbing the pain that prompts her wrath. We get only intimations of an abusive childhood. The lesson here is that female rage is the inevitable result of some disfiguring trauma lodged in the past, as opposed to, say, the systematic oppression that is every woman's present.

*

If Edith was abused as a girl, it becomes much easier to understand her phobic reaction to her daughter's birth, as well as why she would eventually take possession of Grace from her doting father.

But what if she was simply bred into obedience by damaged parents and imagined having a child would salve an otherwise miserable marriage? What if she discovered, upon the baby's arrival, a redoubled sense of entrapment? Wouldn't that be enough to explain her post-partum retreat? Instead, her rejection of Grace becomes her ultimate depravity. What kind of mother can't summon love for *her own baby*?

This question obscures the unsettling truth that *all* women have complicated feelings about motherhood, especially mothers. The rigors of pregnancy, the trauma of child birth, the sleep-deprived tedium of infancy—what sane person wouldn't have qualms? I cop to a certain sensitivity on this subject, because my own mother spent her life processing these feelings as a mother of three children, and as a psychoanalyst. She eventually wrote a book called *The Monster Within* that explores women's fears of giving birth to monsters, which she understood as an extreme expression of maternal ambivalence.

But maternal ambivalence, like feminine rage more broadly, has always been a crime that dare not speak its name, and one therefore spring-loaded with force of its own suppression. Only in the past few decades have novelists begun writing female characters who give voice to their anger, and many, predictably, have had to deal with the literary version of dicklash.

My favorite recent example is Claire Messud's 2014 novel

The Woman Upstairs, a fierce soliloquy delivered by a school teacher named Nora Eldridge. Nora is not one of the "madwomen in the attic" who get so much play, but a dutiful daughter who has spent her entire life muzzling the murder in her heart. "Don't all women feel the same?" she demands. "The only difference is how much we know we feel it, how in touch we are with our fury."

The Woman Upstairs isn't about Nora's anger, though. It's about her despair: "Isn't that always the way, that at the heart of the fire is a frozen kernel of sorrow that the fire is trying—valiantly, fruitlessly—to eradicate."

This sentence crystalizes why the portrayal of Edith Stoner is so unsettling. She's all fire, no kernel. Williams never bothers to explore her sorrow. The probing of the inner life remains a male privilege to the end.

*

I confess that very little of this occurred to me when I first read *Stoner*, because I thought of my own upbringing as enlightened. My parents had met in medical school and both launched careers in psychiatry. On paper, they were equals. But at home, our mother was a second-class citizen: taken for granted, relied upon for domestic labor, often mocked. My professional life, such as it is, has been spent in newsrooms and classrooms where, until recently, there was no talk of gender inequity or diversity. Only in the past few years have I begun to reckon with all this.

More than anything else, my perceptions of the novel have been complicated by the thorny realities of my own marriage.

There was a time, I'm afraid, when I made a habit of pinning our marital strife on the aftershocks of Erin's childhood. I convinced myself that her "trust issues" arose from growing up in a home where she was strictly monitored but never effectively loved, where she didn't feel seen or safe.

It's taken me a dozen years and counting to recognize the truth: that her mistrust is, in large part, a function of my behavior: my self-regard, my efforts to manipulate her, my refusal to accept that her creative work matters as much as my own, that her feelings matter as much as my own, that she has an inner life as rich and complex as my own.

Part of the pleasure I took in reading *Stoner*, frankly, was that it allowed me to indulge in self-pity and dodge culpability. I flattened out my wife just as the novel does. Edith matters only in relation to her husband, first as the object of his fantasy and later a hindrance to his happiness. This is how most female characters function, and how most female humans have been treated.

*

I want to grant here that many readers—myself included—experience the struggles of William Stoner as universal. In this sense, they transcend gender. The novel is about a long and painful marriage, in which one partner has been wounded in ways beyond healing. This is the true story of many marriages, though I would argue that both parties are inevitably damaged to some mysterious extent, and, in the case of heterosexual unions, that men are granted greater license to behave inconsiderately, even destructively, while women are expected to compromise and comply.

I do believe that John Williams struggled to depict Edith Stoner as a person, not a problem. He managed to craft a character unlike any other in all of literature—a roiling id of feminine entrapment. And there are fleeting but distinct moments of empathy toward Edith.

One occurs at the end of a party the Stoners throw for Hollis Lomax, a brilliant and disabled colleague who will become Stoner's second great antagonist. Over the course of the party, Lomax gets drunk and confesses to his loneliness as a child, "the isolation that his deformity had forced upon him, of the early shame which had no source he could understand and no defense that he could muster."

Before leaving, he walks over to Edith to thank her for the party. "Then, as if on a quiet impulse," Williams writes, "he bent a little and touched his lips to hers; Edith's hand came up lightly to touch his hair, and they remained so for several moments while the others looked on. It was the chastest kiss Stoner had ever seen, and it seemed perfectly natural."

I don't know exactly what this gesture means. But I have always suspected that the kiss is one of kinship, that Lomax instinctively recognizes the damage done to Edith during her childhood, the early shame against which *she* can muster no defense.

*

It's important, finally, to acknowledge that the Stoner marriage ends on a note of reconciliation. Williams writes of "a new tranquility" that comes between Stoner and Edith as he lies dying. This quietness, "like the beginning of love," signifies that they have forgiven themselves for their marital failings. Stoner looks at Edith "almost without regret" and her face looks smooth and young in the soft light. "If I had been stronger," he thinks, "if I had known more; if I could have understood. And finally, mercilessly, he thought: if I had loved her more." He reaches out to touch her hand and she allows him to do so, waiting for him to drift off to sleep before withdrawing her hand. Given their history, this qualifies as an unprecedented gesture of tenderness.

The entire scene is astonishing, and it's one I want ardently to believe. One senses Williams attempting to reapportion blame, to suggest that Stoner might somehow have loved Edith into selfhood. Which is kind of bullshit. The problem isn't that Stoner didn't love Edith, but that he never bothered to try to know her.

Williams wants to have it both ways, to consistently portray his hero as entirely powerless, at the mercy of his lunatic wife, but here, right at the end, to proffer Stoner as so noble that he accepts the failure of the marriage as his own. He could have saved his wife. It's arrogance by way of self-effacement. There's also that insinuating modifier: *almost*. *Almost* without regret he looks at her. The word betrays Stoner's reckoning as incomplete. And so many unanswered questions. What was Stoner supposed to understand about Edith? What would more strength have accomplished, or more love?

The novel might well have devoted its energies to those questions, to dismantling Edith Stoner's wrath and examining the world from her perspective, as a woman passed ruthlessly from one man to another and made ruthless in the process. But that novel has yet to be written. And my wife has dibs on it.

5. Everybody Loves a Good Fight

(A Short History of My Many Feuds)

Early in *Stoner*, we track our hero to a local tavern, where he meets each week to drink with two fellow PhD candidates, an affable ass-kisser named Gordon Finch, and Dave Masters, a sly cynic who specializes in the art of brutal assessment. "You, too, are cut out for failure," Master tells Stoner, after a few pints, "not that you'd fight the world. You'd let it chew you up and spit you out, and you'd lie there wondering what was wrong." The comment scans as a bit of drunken banter. But as the novel unfolds, this observation emerges as a central theme: the difficulty of standing up for yourself in the world, the price you pay when you fail to do so, and the price you pay when you succeed.

I can't speak for the rest of you, but I have spent much of my life trying to figure out how to defend my interests in a way that doesn't undo my sanity. Like William Stoner, I have been party to disputes that take shape and escalate without my consent or understanding, that exasperate and exhaust me, so that I often feel as if I, too, am staring up from the ground, wondering what went wrong.

The prophecy of Dave Masters applies most obviously to the Stoner marriage. But no sooner has our hero capitulated to Edith then the novel plunges him into a professional feud, which dominates the second half of the novel. This one is with his cunning colleague, Hollis Lomax, who arrives at the university wreathed in mystery.

His first appearance is at a departmental meeting, to which he arrives conspicuously late. A slow shuffle sounds at the back of the room. Someone whispers, *It's Lomax.* The figure in question is barely five feet and "grotesquely misshapen" with a small hump in his back. His disability makes him appear to be struggling for balance. And yet he is impeccably dressed, right down to the gold cuff links that appear when his right arm shoots out to reveal a lit cigarette, which he puffs dramatically. Only then does he look up, revealing his face, which is that "of a matinee idol. Long and thin and mobile, it was nevertheless strongly featured; his forehead was high and narrow, with heavy veins, and his thick waving hair, the color of ripe wheat, swept back from it in a somewhat theatrical pompadour." Lomax drops his cigarette and grinds it beneath his gleaming wingtips before speaking to his assembled colleagues. "I am Lomax," he tells them, in a booming voice. "I hope I have not disrupted your meeting."

It's one of the most delicious entrances in all of literature: the tension between the deformed body and the dazzling face, the precarious gait and the gestural elegance! Lomax is half Quasimodo, half Cary Grant, with an advanced degree in malicious drama. In other words, he's perfectly cast as a foil to William Stoner, a man stolid down to his inanimate surname.

But the pair don't start out as enemies. On the contrary, Stoner is drawn to Lomax, whose eloquence reminds him of Dave Masters. A friendship seems imminent, especially after the Stoners throw a party where a drunken Lomax, before applying that chaste kiss to Edith, speaks of his solitude and how literature rescued him. Stoner sees that Lomax has gone through the same kind of conversion he experienced in class with Archer Sloane. At school, he greets Lomax warmly, expecting kinship, but he is met with "an irony that was like cold anger." Unwittingly, Stoner has again intruded upon the privacy of a damaged person. Lomax is ashamed of having exposed himself and converts this shame into enmity.

Their grudge begins when Lomax's protégé, a disabled graduate student named Charles Walker, wheedles his way into one of Stoner's graduate seminars. Walker shows up late for the next class, in a clumsy imitation of his mentor. He then interrupts the lecture incessantly.

Stoner is concerned enough to consult Lomax, who looks directly at Stoner and says, "with cheerful malevolence, 'As you may have noticed, he is a cripple.'" By the end of their chat, Lomax's voice is trembling with anger. Stoner can see that his colleague has personalized the situation. But he does not see—and the reader must therefore see on his behalf—that Lomax has begun laying a trap for him, one in which Walker is merely the bait.

Walker continues to act out. When the other students ignore him, he retreats into a mood of "outraged integrity." He delays his presentation and a young instructor named Katherine Driscoll delivers a dazzling paper in his stead. Stoner arrives at the next class to find Walker seated at his desk, clearly fantasizing about replacing him as professor. Walker's paper is actually an improvised performance, a garish imitation of Lomax unrelated to his proposed subject. It is devoted, instead, to denigrating Katherine Driscoll's work.

After class, Stoner apologizes to Katherine. She can barely restrain her laughter, for she can see the obvious truth—that Walker was attacking Stoner, not her. Stoner orders Walker to turn over the text of his presentation, though it's clear no such text exists. When Walker refuses, Stoner informs him he will fail the class. "One must be prepared to suffer for one's beliefs," Walker declares.

"'And for one's laziness and dishonesty and ignorance,'" Stoner snaps. He goes on to suggest that Walker re-examine his position at the university, and whether he has any place in a graduate program.

*

It's one of those moments where you want pat old Stoner on the back; he's finally brought the hammer down on this arrogant provocateur. At the same time, one senses, queasily, that he's been played by Lomax. This feeling of exhilarated dread, of knowing we're headed for a nasty showdown (a feeling that deserves its own complicated German word) is part of what makes *Stoner* so irresistible.

Word soon arrives that Stoner will have to serve on the committee overseeing Walker's oral exams, alongside his advisor … Lomax. What follows is a ten-page set piece in which a discussion of medieval literature goes medieval. Walker, though dazzling when discussing his dissertation, knows nothing of the required texts. Stoner watches, with a grim and growing sense of duty, as Lomax deftly manipulates the conversation to obscure his protégé's glaring deficits.

When it's finally his turn, Stoner asks Walker a series of remedial questions about the literary tradition. The candidate flusters and filibusters. Lomax tries to interrupt but Stoner calmly shuts down these efforts. "I am asking simple questions," he says. "I must insist upon simple answers."

There is a giddy pleasure to all this—the pleasure of watching a slick fraud exposed in real time. And I might as well confess that chewing over this scene in the age of Donald Trump yields an especially piquant vision of vindication. If only the moderators at one of the 2016 presidential debates had exhibited the courage to follow Stoner's example! Had asked Trump to recite the duties of the presidency as outlined in the Constitution. Or the contents of the Thirteenth Amendment. Or the Nineteenth Amendment. Or to summarize the outcome of the Dred Scot case. Or the tenets of the Monroe Doctrine. Or to identify the components of the nuclear triad. Or to identify the tax rate for the wealthiest Americans under President Eisenhower. If only they had refused to allow the candidate to hide behind the bombastic talking points cribbed from talk radio. *I am asking simple questions, Mr. Trump. I must insist upon simple answers.*

Anyway.

The questioning goes on until Stoner's disgust gives way to "a kind of pity and sick regret." Walker doesn't even know the poems of the Romantic period, his alleged specialty. Stoner votes to fail him, naturally. Lomax is apoplectic. "Do you realize what you're doing to the boy?" he shouts.

"I'm preventing him from teaching in a college or university," Stoner replies. "Which is precisely what I want to do." For him, this dispute is about nothing less than the intellectual purity of the academy.

The problem, as Masters warned him years ago, is that the purity of the academy is a mirage. Lomax wastes no time proving the case. He threatens to bring formal charges against Stoner. When this plan fails, he flexes his power as chair of the English Department. Lomax saddles his rival with a nightmare schedule, blocks his academic progress, and prevents him from teaching courses in his specialty. Walker returns to campus, strutting about like a conquering hero and openly mocking Stoner. Lomax makes no secret of the feud and it soon pollutes the entire department.

When Stoner implores Lomax to relent, he receives as his response an aria of projective rage. Lomax believes, with utter sincerity, that Stoner has tried to ruin Walker's career. And not just because of Walker's "enthusiasm and integrity" but because of "an unfortunate physical affliction that would have called forth sympathy in a normal human being."

Williams captures something here that lies at the heart of all conflict: our unconscious compulsion to project onto our enemies the most intractable aspects of our self-hatred. For all his powers of intellect, Lomax feels monstrous. Thus, he tells himself a story in which Stoner is the monster, the man who falls short of normalcy. Some part of Lomax knows that his defense of Walker has desecrated his professional integrity. And this too, winds up projected onto Stoner. "I don't think you're fit to be a teacher," he seethes. "No man is, whose prejudices override his talent and his learning."

This encounter is the last time the two men will speak for twenty years. Before Stoner departs, he takes a last look at the man he once hoped to befriend. Lomax stares at the papers on his desk. His face is red, and he appears to be struggling with himself. Stoner suddenly realizes what he's witnessing: not anger but shame.

*

I've always loved this scene for its unflinching portrayal of Lomax, in particular this moment when his shame comes into view. But to revisit this exchange in the America of this moment is to recognize the enormity of shame as a driving force in our political discourse. It's always been there, of course, simmering beneath the moral atrocities of our history. "There is no greater injustice than to wring your profits from the sweat of another man's brow," Lincoln insisted. You slave owners should be ashamed of yourselves. That's what he was saying.

A century and a half later, Donald Trump brought the Party of Lincoln to the opposite conclusion: that being a white man in America means never having to say you're sorry. No public figure in our history has exploited shame so relentlessly. The beating heart of his candidacy was not his command of policy or his oratory or even the moneyed gloss of his celebrity. It was his instinctive ability to weaponize the inner life of his partisans, to transmute the shame of their bigotry and declining utility and angry dependence into a cleansing rage.

The pundits and pollsters missed this altogether. Every time he said or did something despicable, a chorus of condemnation rang out, which allowed Trump to cast himself as the injured party, forever smeared by a cabal of condescending elites. Like Lomax, Trump feuds not as a strategy but as a compulsion, a way of recasting his sadistic urges as a necessary, even noble, defense against the judgment of others.

William Monahan captures the mindset precisely in his novel *The Lighthouse*: "Like most evil, self-interested people, Mr. Glowery thought (it may actually be a form innocence) that everyone else was as evil and self-interested as he was, and that no matter what he did to harm other people, he was merely protecting himself intelligently against enemies as obsessive as himself. Mr. Glowery really believed that everyone did this sort of thing constantly."

The revelation of 2016 was that Americans became completely mesmerized by *this sort of thing*. The media covered Trump obsessively because Trump obsessively feuded. In a mature democracy, each election is a contest of ideas. Ours are about feuds, locking a woman up, punching someone out. People tune into politics today for the same reason they tune into reality TV or social media or mixed martial arts: for the blood and the shame.

I've thought a good deal about this peculiar national lust and concluded that Americans are conflict junkies precisely because we spend so much of our psychic energy avoiding conflict. This is what makes us vulnerable to trolls, whether they dwell in a basement or the Oval Office: they enact our stifled impulses.

Edith and Lomax dominate Stoner in the same way demagogues dominate their political opponents; not through superior ideas or logic, but the seductive force of uninhibited aggression. This is the secret sauce modern conservatives use to advance a plutocratic and bigoted agenda. At a primal level, they project a willingness to fight.

If John Kerry had turned to George W. Bush during any of their presidential debates and said, "In 1969, I was on the Duong Keo River killing Vietcong and watching my friends bleed out. Where were you in 1969?" he would have been elected president. Just as Hillary Clinton would be president today if, during her second debate with Trump, she had turned to him and said: "Stop stalking me around the stage. It doesn't make you look tough, Donald. It makes you look like a creep who harrasses women."

But look: that's not who liberals are. They don't punch bullies. They go high, like Stoner, and wind up on the ground wondering what went wrong.

It is worth noting here that Williams was inspired to write *Stoner* by a legendary row between two senior professors in his department. And that he composed much of the book while embroiled in a feud with his hero, the combative poet and critic Yvor Winters, who accused Williams of plagiarism and threatened to destroy his reputation. Williams must have felt what his protagonist does: that a potential friend had become a dogged adversary, one who, based on the archival record, gleefully leveraged his aggression into dominance.

*

For the past four years, I've been the co-host of a strange and rather beautiful podcast called "Dear Sugars," which consists of me and my friend, the writer Cheryl Strayed, answering letters from people in crisis. Our in-box contains thousands of stories. It's more or less a transcription of the culture's inner life. Regardless of what the letters detail—death, abuse, infidelity, motherhood, friendship—nearly all include an element of conflict avoidance. Our correspondents know they need to confront someone in their lives but they haven't worked up the courage, so they write to us instead. They're in conflict about conflict.

I've spent my entire life in this state. I was bullied in school and at home and spent much of my waking life fantasizing about fighting back. My brothers and I brawled, rather ineptly, but never resolved the resentments that led to the punches. To this day, more than forty years on, I can remember those scuffles: the indignation I felt at my older brother yanking me into a headlock by my hair, me socking him in the jaw the moment he freed me, my father sitting on a piano bench watching all this, urging me stand up to my brother. That was the fight, I believe, in which Dave broke his hand punching my skull.

I remember tussling with my twin brother, too, both of us standing at the foot of a bed huffing with adrenaline, not knowing what was going to happen next. Then I heard a loud slap and saw Mike was holding his cheek and for a long moment I had no idea that my hand had flown up and struck him.

The emotional violence was worse. My brothers forged a closer bond with each other than with me, and I never forgave them for that. They broke me once, hurling down insults from the second floor of some vacation condo until I wept right in front of them. I spent the next two decades unconsciously chasing the same degradation.

I didn't want to fight at all. On the other hand, all I

wanted to do was fight. I felt like a bloodhound circling my own aggression. I can remember being at a heavy metal show shortly after college when a brawl broke out. I leapt into the middle of the scrum to play peacemaker. But the moment I saw the horror on my date's face I realized I'd been drawn by the promise of violence. Like a lot of men, I told the world I was the sensitive kind, a lover not a fighter, then snuck off to watch football games and boxing matches where I could feed on the brutality of other men, asking myself all the while: was I going to stand up for myself?

*

Stoner was a part of this. It was asking the same question: whether the hero would ever punch back. The novel found me, as I've mentioned, in my first year of graduate school, thanks to a friend. But the original source was actually one of our teachers, whom I'll call Professor X. He was in every respect a rising star: young, handsome, charming. A glowing *New York Times* review of his debut story collection had been taped to the door of the director's office and I read this notice in awe. I hoped he would like my work and become my mentor, perhaps even my friend.

I worked hard to win his favor in workshop, writing detailed critiques of the stories submitted by my colleagues and eagerly participating in class discussions. And then, one day, Professor X asked me to stop by his office after class. I was certain—in the way aspiring disciples are always certain—that our special bond was about to be consecrated.

Instead, Professor X sat me down and chided me for

speaking too harshly in class about another student's work. I apologized, instantly and earnestly. I felt it was still possible that this reprimand was a kind of formality, and that the true purpose of the visit was to recognize my efforts in class. But Professor X continued to glare at me. After a few long and embarrassing seconds, I laughed softly. "I get it," I said. "I screwed up." I can now see that this was just the wrong thing to do, that my effort to defuse tension had registered as disrespect.

I don't mean to portray myself as an angel. I was ambitious and insecure, always a volatile mix, and because I had come from the world of journalism—and before that, Judaism—my manner registered as brash. I was also sad and lonesome at that time in my life, and often drove people away from me without realizing why. But mostly, looking back, I can see that I was naïve. Like William Stoner, I viewed the academy as a refuge from the competitive clashes of the newsroom.

My unconscious expectations were even more outlandish. I wanted my professors to enforce empathy in a way my parents never managed, to keep us creative siblings from turning on each other. Professor X wasn't like that. Despite his scolding, he allowed students to argue with each other and sometimes criticized other writers in front of us. Before one class, he abruptly announced that we wouldn't be discussing a particular manuscript because it was unworthy of our consideration. The woman who had written the story sat there, absorbing this humiliation. She called me in tears that night, and left the program altogether within a few months.

A few days after the term ended, Professor X called me at home. This was before the age of cell phones, so I didn't know it was him until his voice filled my ear. I was excited, because I still believed that he recognized my dedication and wanted to be my mentor. That was why he was calling me *at home*!

That was not why he was calling me at home. He was calling to berate me, which he did for several minutes. He told me that I was a loose cannon and that I didn't respect him and that he wouldn't read my thesis work if I didn't shape up.

All through that broiling summer I perseverated on this conversation, trying to figure out how I had provoked such wrath. I shaved my head, too, in some kind of penitential fit. My nose was suddenly huge and my skull was a pale bulb nicked and seamed with scars from those ancient fights with my brothers.

*

When I returned to campus in the fall, I found a home-made cassette tape in my mailbox—made by Professor X—with a note saying he looked forward to reading my thesis. It was a peace offering, and I was glad to have it. Also in my mailbox was a note from the Chair of the English Department announcing that Professor X was up for tenure, and soliciting students to write letters for his file. It never occurred to me, until just now, that these two items might be related. I thought Professor X just felt bad for hollering at me.

The request for letters urged us to be "absolutely candid" and I took this to mean that our letters would not be shared with Professor X. I wrote an absolutely candid letter. I acknowledged that Professor X was an outstanding teacher to most of his students, but that I could only speak to my own experiences, which I then detailed.

It would be lovely to suppose that I wrote this letter solely at the bidding of my conscience, that, like Stoner, I had the sanctity of the academy in mind. But I want to be honest about my motives here: I was ravenous for revenge. Professor X had abused his power. That was how I saw it.

Within the week, Professor X left a second note in my mailbox stating that he would not be reading my thesis. No explanation was necessary; clearly, my letter had not been confidential. In fact, we never spoke another word to one another. Our feud infected the entire program. A palpable tension swirled when we were in the same room. He was awarded tenure. But the general perception—one I was only dimly aware of amid my blinding sense of persecution—was that I'd tried to torpedo his career.

The other fiction writer on the faculty eventually announced that she, too, wouldn't read my thesis. I can remember walking across campus in a torrential rain and seeing this woman, a former teacher of mine, walking towards me. We were the only two people in sight. Rather than pass by me, she veered off the path and into a bog of muddy lawn. I watched all this in a kind of wonder, her dress shoes tugged at by the mud, her face red with what I can now see was shame.

I grew isolated and depressed and read *Stoner* a third time, then a fourth. The book had found me only because of Professor X, though I'm not sure the irony of the situation would have impressed me.

It's been more than two decades since I left my graduate program and I still have no idea why Professor X personalized our relationship. I do know that he was struggling during those years in ways that were mostly hidden from view, drinking too much, splitting up with his wife. He was a young guy under a lot of pressure, having to teach a bunch of students who essentially wanted his job. He probably saw me as a threat to his legitimacy. But that's just a guess.

I do know that we looked strikingly similar, so much so that people would sometimes get us mixed up, and that Professor X had the same name as my twin brother. My own desperation for his approval no doubt dated back to my childhood, and invoked an ancient sense of victimhood, of powerlessness, that I must have provoked in ways I still can't see. The whole reason we stage feuds—whether personal or political—is to blind ourselves with rage.

In the end, I had to ask professors outside the program to read my thesis. One of those poor souls, a poet, wrote to express his confusion about the epigraph, a quote from a Steve Earle song that had nothing to do with the stories themselves, and would have made no sense to anyone but me and Professor X:

> *I got a razor in my pocket*
> *I got a razor in my pocket*
> *I got a razor in my pocket*
> *And a pistol hid down by the school*

*

I wish I could report that my feuding days ended there. But over the past two decades I've racked up a stunning roster of rivals: literary agents and fellow writers, publishers, bloggers, and professional demagogues. A complete archive of my feuds would extend from the folder in my inbox labeled "Crazy Shit" to the archives of Fox News.

I'm pretty sure I enjoy the distinction of being the only author ever to have to be physically separated from his own publisher at Book Expo. This would have been in 2006. The publisher had cornered me backstage after a book signing and demanded that I interact with her, something I did not wish to do because she was, in my estimation, an inept lunatic.

After the Expo, this publisher called me repeatedly, insisting that we needed to resolve our issues. Her conscious motive was to work things out—I give her that credit. But it was also clear that her pride had been injured and so she wanted, also, to reaffirm her own power, to get back into it with me, to *do the dance*. This is the term of art I use when I can sense that someone is itching to feud with me.

I knew I'd have to do the dance with her eventually, and that when I did she would try to reignite our rancor. So I wrote a script for myself. The script said this: "I know we've had our differences in the past, but I'm confident we'll be able to work together moving forward." When at last we talked on the phone, this was literally the only thing I said.

Publisher: "We need to be able to talk about what happened at the Expo, Steve."

Me: "I know we've had our differences in the past, but I'm confident we'll be able to work together moving forward."

Publisher: "I've never been treated that way by another writer."

Me: "I know we've had our differences in the past, but I'm confident we'll be able to work together moving forward."

Publisher: "I don't understand why you're so angry."

Me: "I know we've had our differences in the past, but I'm confident we'll be able to work together moving forward."

On and on it went, until my publisher, having passed through provocation and antic rage into a kind of exhausted futility, hung up.

I thought I'd won. I bounced around my apartment. I called my best friend to recount the triumph. But no one wins in a feud, especially when you beef with someone more powerful than you. That's the whole point of *Stoner*. In this case, the publisher decided not to put out a paperback edition of my next book, damning it to an even more certain obscurity.

6. The Perfect Martyr

The foregoing chapter should make two facts pretty obvious:

1. Most of *Stoner* is about a guy getting pummeled.
2. The author of this book is somewhat pathologically inclined toward feuds.

These two facts are intimately bound. The *Stoner* saga represents a wish fantasy for readers such as me precisely because we take pleasure in identifying with William Stoner as an entirely innocent victim—the perfect martyr.

Stoner always acts with pure intentions. He woos Edith with an abject devotion and reacts to her obvious dissatisfactions by redoubling his efforts to please her. He courts Lomax with the same guileless determination and winds up sandbagged by an implacable antagonist. There is nothing Stoner can do to defuse these folks—nothing within the capacities of his character, anyway. Thus he suffers, extravagantly, exuding the quiet dignity of the persecuted. The battles exhaust and depress him. Yet he never surrenders to cynicism or complaint or even apathy, not once. He carries on with his sacred calling.

If you're sniffing something distinctly Christic in the saga, that is by authorial design. "The point of the novel," Williams explained to his agent, "will be that [Stoner] is a kind of saint."

Stoner himself is wholly unaware of his sanctification.

He's too busy dodging Edith's slings and grading freshman compositions in the gloom of his office. Thus, the reader is granted the strange pleasure of marveling at his stoicism, a pleasure intensified by the particular features of the modern American inner life.

What do I mean here? I mean that our cultural posture has become one of perpetual complaint. (Note: this observation is itself a *complaint*.) As citizens of history's most rabid capitalist cult, we have come of age in a society that profits by making us feel insecure and impatient. We are awash in images of lives more prosperous and pleasurable than our own—luxury hotel suites, pornographic tacos, sun-struck highways.

And thus, as we trudge through a reality of grubby rooms and digestive malfunction and snarls of traffic, we are highly susceptible to the belief that we have been wronged. This is a dominant feeling among our citizens: a virulent self-pity that has been eagerly (and lucratively) cultivated into a booming political and media market.

As I write this, our nation has just witnessed the mass murder of eleven Jews at a synagogue in Pittsburgh. Hours before the shooter went on his rampage, he went online to share his motive, which centered on a Jewish nonprofit that provides aid to refugees. He believed this organization "likes to bring invaders in that kill our people. I can't sit by and watch my people get slaughtered. Screw your optics, I'm going in."

He was convinced that this humanitarian group had infiltrated a "caravan" of central Americans fleeing violence in their own countries and traveling north, toward the United States. In other words, he saw a bunch of hungry, tired refugees, most of them women and children, as an advancing army. Why?

Because a raft of paid demagogues and political actors had been spouting this anti-Semitic conspiracy theory for weeks.

He wasn't *convinced* in the passive voice. That's a copout. Specific people, one of them our president, actively convinced this man that he was the true victim, and that only by slaughtering a bunch of Jewish strangers at their weekly religious services would he be able to keep *his people safe*. This is how terrorists think. They always see themselves as martyrs whose rampages are principled and heroic.

In Trump's America, this kind of lethal paranoia is no longer quarantined to the cultural margins. It is the ethos of a major political party and the default setting of a population addicted to victimization. Every issue—from taxation to immigration to religious rights—is now routinely framed as a victim drama. The fixation on gun ownership is, at root, an obsession with victimization. Only unfettered access to assault rifles will keep *our people safe*. Only the gun lobby will protect us from the gun grabbers. Even the debate over something as practical as affordable healthcare becomes a victim drama if you can convince people that a bill intended to make insurance more affordable will include government death panels.

Is it any wonder that half the films churned out by Hollywood are comic book epics that portray a cosmos organized into villainy and victimhood?

*

I realize I have wandered off the reservation of literary tribute again and into the morass of public morality. But I'm after something here, which is the peculiar and pervasive gratification that we all feel, as humans, when we connect to our own sense of victimhood.

In the case of the conspiracy theorist, that victimhood is energetically constructed from a set of stray facts and insinuations, bound by the feverish logic of paranoia. Stoner himself encounters this pattern of thought in the outbreak of McCarthyism, which he rightly diagnoses as a form of mental illness. "He saw hatred and suspicion become a kind of madness that swept the land like a swift plague."

Such mass contagions thrive in frightened and fractious eras, but they are predicated on a timeless susceptibility, a dire need to regard ourselves as the central victim in any story. This delusion, however cynically promoted, arises from a real set of fears: that we are at the mercy of forces beyond our control.

Literature often functions as a balm to such anxieties by focusing on figures who specialize in overcoming adversity and shaping their own destiny. David Copperfield pondered whether he would be the hero of his own story, after all, not the victim.

But there is an even more ancient tradition to consider. Martyrs are central to and inextricable from our religious mythology: we have only to think of figures such as Job and Christ whose grotesque suffering is exalted as the central proof of their devotion. William Stoner is a throwback to such figures. He is born poor. He dedicates himself to an obscure mission. He eschews egoism and is dependably punished for his virtues. He acquiesces to unprincipled enemies and suffers without complaint. In a characterological sense, he is literally the anti-Trump. Bearing witness to his relentless integrity is a kind of fetish for *Stonerians*, a secular version of religious faith.

But there's also a crucial element of escapism at work. The novel portrays a world in which those determined to antagonize Stoner always find a way, and his efforts to avoid that antagonism are therefore doomed. He cannot defuse his rivals. Thus, every time I read *Stoner*, I am briefly and thrillingly convinced that the same applies to me.

It doesn't. Because let's face it: we *always* collaborate in the creation and perpetuation of our feuds. They arise in response to our particular cycles of idealization and disappointment. They escalate because both parties come to believe they are protecting something sacred. They boil over because we suppress our frustrations and thereby condense them into wrath. We then compound the crisis by underestimating our power in relation to our rivals.

*

As an example, let me revisit another dispute with a publisher, for whom I wrote a book about the moral atrocities of football. The central point of contention between us was the cover that would grace this volume. I wanted an image reflective of my radical position—ideally, a photo that captured the savagery at the heart of the enterprise. The publisher favored an image without violence, which his sales team feared would alienate female readers.

Soon, the dispute had gone beyond the cover. It was about us, our egos, the trench warfare of trust and respect. My job was to write the book. His job was to decide how the book would be presented to the world. He needed me to understand that he held the power. This was why he disregarded a series of emails and phone calls, a pattern I found humiliating.

When I finally exploded, I made sure to inflict maximum humiliation. I told him that I had decided to work with him because I thought he truly cared about art and social justice, that he wasn't just a corporate suit who answered to the folks in marketing. I implied that he was the very thing he had spent his life attempting to prove he wasn't: a sellout. I also assailed his power by announcing that I would have nothing further to do with the book if he insisted on a cover I didn't approve of, and that I was happy to return my advance and shop the book elsewhere if he had a problem with that.

I will spare you the arias of rage that followed because I never actually heard them. The publisher did put the book out, but he never spoke another word to me, dispatching under-lings to carry out that odious task.

Was I intransigent? Out of line? Even sadistic?

Yeah, I guess I was.

And yet, when I go back over the steps that led to this falling out, I don't see how we could have avoided it. He was always going to impose his agenda as a publisher, which I was always going to experience as bullying. I was always going to lash out at him, which was always going to infuriate him. We were always going to do this particular dance because we were programmed, long ago, to do so.

*

I saw myself as the doomed hero in this scenario, the trampled artist. There is something in me—that residue of having been bullied as a kid, of struggling to control my own aggression—that bristles when I sense someone trying to roll me. I latch onto offenses, overt or perceived. I nurture my victim status and use it as a justification for high-handed literary attacks.

To indulge in a meta moment, I'll point out what has no doubt occurred to many of you: the very act of writing about all these feuds is, at least in part, prompted by a desire to reignite them. This is how it works with us perfect martyrs: combat is our form of intimacy, our path back to the place where the pain began. Consciously, we want to punish other people. Unconsciously, we want to punish ourselves.

And this does actually steer me back to William Stoner, whose martyrdom arises from a bottomless well of masochism. Nearly every decision he makes over the course of the novel— to woo and marry Edith Stoner, to surrender his daughter to her care, to withstand Lomax's assaults—causes him distress.

But don't talk my word for it. Toward the end of the novel, Grace visits her dying father. "Poor daddy," she says, "things haven't been easy for you, have they?"

"No," Stoner responds. "But I suppose I didn't want them to be."

I shouldn't be heartened by these words. But I always am. It's so rare to encounter a person, even a fictional person, who can cop to his masochism. Most of us walk around doing everything we can to not recognize the ways in which we conspire against ourselves. We pretend that our central desire is always contentment. It's not. Our central desire is to feel alive in the ways that are most familiar to us. In this sense, as we'll see further on, Stoner has no precedent for the joy he finds in literature and teaching. His childhood has prepared him only for a life of agricultural hardship. He has make things hard for himself.

But it's also true that he finds ways to contend with his tormentors over the course of the novel. After years of being an exile who basically lives on campus, for instance, Stoner returns home. Edith goes nuts, but this time Stoner refuses to acknowledge her provocations, and she finally accepts his presence.

His response to Lomax's academic abuses is ingenious: he begins teaching his freshman comp classes as if they were the advanced seminars over which he once presided. Rather than primers on rhetoric, he assigns his students sophisticated texts on medieval English. Lomax tries to intercede but Stoner cheerfully notes that it would be dangerous to interfere with the teaching method of a senior faculty member. Outwitted, Lomax hands his rival the classes he should have been teaching all along.

Stoner takes no great pleasure in these triumphs. He just wants what he's due. That's what I genuinely admire: the humility with which Stoner navigates his misfortune. He comes to understand that the world and its wounded are going to come after you, and that you have to find ways to defend yourself without doing the dance.

Reading *Stoner* makes me wish I were better at that. I regret all the hours I've squandered defending my honor when I should have been asserting my rights, and working to accept the limits of my power in the world. William Stoner's dignity makes me feel undignified. To put it more gently: beholding his virtue has brought me closer to a version of myself I can stand.

At the same time, I've learned a good deal from *Stoner* about the excesses of self-sacrifice, especially in the context of my personal life. In my marriage, and even more so as a parent, I've caught myself engaging in a pattern of feverish and reflexive service to my children, sanctifying their happiness while ignoring my own. Not only does this foster ingratitude and entitlement within them, it turns me into a guilt-provoking schmuck, the kind of dad who volunteers to drive his daughter to school on a rainy day (as I did just this morning) then says to her just before she gets out of the car, and in true drama queen style, "Gee dad, thanks for taking time away from your work to give me a ride!"

In this case, miraculously, my daughter did thank me. It was a lovely moment. But it had the fingerprints of the perfect martyr all over it. Generosity isn't supposed to be transactional, after all. It shouldn't come with a receipt of assumed victimhood. What I'm getting at here is that there is no such thing as a perfect martyr because life isn't a suffering pageant. It should be possible—even for modern parents—to move beyond the role of "poor daddy" (or poor mommy), to ease the burdens of their children without making things hard for themselves.

7. Studies in Class

It would be lovely to present *Stoner* as a novel purely devoted to the inner life. It would also be inaccurate. The book is also very much about the material world, about the collision of poverty and privilege, which is to say about class. It took me half a dozen readings to realize how persistently Williams explores this theme. He takes a far more subtle approach than, say, Dickens. But he's equally resolute.

This is why the earliest pages of the book are dedicated to an unflinching description of the Stoner family farm. It's an operation "bound together by the necessity of its toil," with a crude homestead that has taken on the colors of the parched land around it, and floors "of unpainted plank, unevenly spaced and cracking with age, up through which dust steadily seeped and was swept back each day by Stoner's mother." His parents are described as nearly insensate, enslaved to an unforgiving earth that seems forever on the verge of swallowing them up.

John Williams did not grow up on such a farm. But the circumstances into which he was born were indisputably meager. His biological father died under nefarious circumstances—or, just as likely, abandoned his family—when Williams was three, and his mother remarried a heavy drinker who couldn't keep the rent paid. The family eventually sought refuge with his mother's people, farmers in Clarksville, Texas.

Williams was an early reader, and went on to become a dedicated academic and author. But his erudition provoked more skepticism than pride in his kin, and the dandy clothes he later donned as a professor, as well as the cigarette holder, should be viewed not as a mark of his breeding, but a desire to compensate for the conditions of his youth.

Stoner, then, isn't just a story of a literary awakening. It's also about the fraught journey from a life of subsistence to one of relative abundance, about what it's like to betray your legacy even as you seek your destiny.

This tension is bound to the novel's instigating event: the visit from the county agent who suggests that William attend college. In response, Stoner's father delivers what we are told is the longest speech of his life. He observes that he "never held with schooling" when he was young, but that his land has grown harder to work; he acknowledges what the county agent has told him: that his son might learn new methods of farming at the University. "Maybe he's right," the senior Stoner observes. "Sometimes when I'm out in the field I get to thinking."

It's a moment where we can see, fleetingly, the stirring of his imagination, which fixes on adaptation as a necessity. He sends his only son off to college not to pursue self-improvement, but as a means of familial survival.

Stoner travels by foot and buggy to Columbia and arrives at the university covered in red dirt. He gazes at the grand brick buildings and fields of green in awe; he can bring himself to do no more than pace the edges of the campus. He boards with an elderly couple who work a farm outside of the city. The Footes are cousins to Stoner but regard the young scholar with suspicion, scoffing at his academic ambitions and happily exploiting his labor. His room has no heat, and in winter he has to wrap himself in ragged blankets and blow on his hands so he can turn the pages of his books without tearing them.

These privations are understood by all parties as the punishment inflicted on those who seek to rise above their station. Indeed, one of the most notable symptoms of Stoner's decision to study and teach literature is that he feels empowered to reject this treatment. In this sense, his revelation registers as triumphant.

But the novel refuses to dodge the underside of this heroism: the crushing betrayal he visits upon his parents, who have sacrificed so much to send him to college. The whole point of his schooling, so far as they are concerned, is for him to rescue the farm, not to abandon it. Stoner is so plagued by guilt that he hides his decision for years. On the morning of his graduation, he glances at his folks, "the brown faces that rose nakedly out of their new clothing," and his will fails him yet again.

When he finally confesses, his father assumes he's has gotten himself into some kind of trouble. Stoner attempts to explain his plan to teach; his father receives the words "as a stone receives the repeated blows of a fist." His mother's reaction is to squeeze her eyes shut and breathe heavily and press her fists against her cheeks. "With wonder Stoner realized that she was crying, deeply and silently, with the shame and awkwardness of one who seldom weeps."

To pursue his future, Stoner must cut ties with his past. He becomes both orphan and traitor and spends the rest of his days haunted by a secret sense of his own wrongdoing. This is why he engineers situations designed to punish himself.

*

The most obvious and vexing example is his decision to court and marry Edith Bostwick. Given that Stoner has, to this point in his life, expressed no romantic inclinations, it is worth pondering why he is transfixed by Edith. Stoner is teaching at a large university where, presumably, they are women he might find intellectually and temperamentally compatible. So why Edith?

Her beauty plays a role. But it is a beauty bound up in Stoner's particular ideas about grace and refinement, which is to say class. He meets her at a reception held in "the grandest house" he has ever been near, spotting her at the head of a massive walnut table "covered with yellow damask and laden with white dishes and bowls of gleaming silver." As she delicately pours tea into gold-rimmed cups, Stoner is "assailed by a consciousness of his own heavy clumsiness."

This initial view is enough to spur an ardor worthy of Gatsby: "There must have been moments even that afternoon when Daisy tumbled short of his dreams—not through her own fault, but because of the colossal vitality of his illusion. It had gone beyond her, beyond everything."

Stoner wants the same thing: to possess a woman who personifies wealth and punishes him for repudiating his birthright. The more we learn about the Bostwick family, the more obvious this becomes. Horace is a banker by profession and a pompous charlatan by nature, covetous in spirit and corpulent in form. His wife exhibits a bitterness "so general and pervasive that no specific remedy" can assuage it.

During the pre-marital interview, she peers at Stoner "curiously, as if his face were smudged or his nose were bleeding," while Horace is dismayed to learn that his daughter's suitor has no means beyond his profession. He points out that Edith has had "advantages" such as a fine home and servants and private schools, and wonders out loud how she will survive the reduced standard sure to be inflicted by what he calls Stoner's "condition."

Stoner is so humiliated he's ready to rescind his proposal.

The reader expects Bostwick to be relieved. Instead, he turns panicky and deferential. His bluff has been called. He knows that his daughter is ill-prepared for the duties of adulthood; beneath his bluster he's desperate to marry her off.

Stoner's own father recognizes the situation instantly. Upon meeting Edith, he stares directly into her eyes and issues a shockingly candid challenge. "A man needs himself a woman, to do for him and give him comfort. Now you be good to William. He ought to have someone who can be good to him."

"I'll try Mr. Stoner," comes Edith's doomed rejoinder. "I'll try."

*

The entirety of Stoner's marriage can be thought of as one long and bruising lesson in the pathologies of class. Edith has been "educated upon the premise that she would be protected from the gross events that life might thrust in her way, and upon the premise that she had no other duty than to be a graceful and accomplished accessory to that protection, since she belonged to a social and economic class to which protection was an almost sacred obligation."

Cosseted by her privilege, Edith is unprepared for the gross events that marriage and motherhood require. In defiance of the prevailing gender norms, Stoner becomes her indentured servant. He's up before dawn, grading papers, preparing lectures, feeding wife and daughter, and cleaning their apartment. Then he rushes off to his teaching job. Edith responds by chastising him for being unable to furnish her a proper home. She insists that she can't live in an apartment because of the noise made by her husband and her child. Worst of all, she's forced to smell the baby. This monstrous entitlement is a direct result of her wealth, the fact that Edith has never had to care for herself, even one day of her life. "Nor could it ever have occurred to her that she might become responsible for the well-being of another."

Stoner argues, explicitly and persistently, that the pursuit and acquisition of wealth represents a corruption of the spirit. It comes as no surprise that Horace Bostwick takes his own life days after the crash of 1929, having made ruinous decisions with other people's money, like his disgraced father.

After the funeral, Edith embarks on a new project: reinventing herself. This involves purchasing a new wardrobe, painting her face, smoking cigarettes, and cultivating a European accent. Stoner, meanwhile, dedicates himself to his daughter and his teaching. As he sands down planks of wood for a new bookcase he notices "the roughness of the surface disappearing … it was himself he was making possible." When Edith returns home, she recognizes at once that it is her husband, and not she, who has undergone a genuine transformation.

This is the template of their marriage: Stoner places his faith in hard work and a halting introspection. Edith collects affectations and attempts to drown her boredom in empty materialism. She's incapable of psychic growth. When Stoner fails Charles Walker, provoking Lomax's wrath, Edith's reaction travels to the heart of her essential amorality. She notes that they've been poor so far, and that they'll carry on being poor. What she can't understand is why her husband insists on defending his principles. "What *difference* could it make?" she mutters.

Her response to Grace's pregnancy is even more striking: "Oh, my God. Oh, Gracie. How could you—oh, my God. Like your father. Your father's blood. Oh, yes. Filth. Filth—" Here at last Edith reveals the blood libel that has governed their entire marriage.

It is one that Stoner well recognizes, for "deep in him, beneath his memory" is an awareness of his origins. He rarely thinks of his early years on the farm outside Boonville, but the "blood knowledge of his inheritance" pervades his consciousness, a knowledge bequeathed to him by "forefathers whose lives were obscure and hard and stoical and whose common ethic was to present to an oppressive world faces that were expressionless and hard and bleak."

Edith's bigotry takes root in the very soil of his character.

*

The novel's preoccupation with class extends well beyond a toxic homestead. Stoner is aware of the age in which he lives, and inwardly devastated by the effects of the Great Depression, which he witnesses unfolding around him. He sees the vacant faces of men whose vision of a decent life have been shattered, and are thus left to wander the streets and skulk up to back doors to "beg for the bread that would allow them to beg again." Stoner recognizes the perch of his own privilege, as well. "He saw men," Williams writes, "who had once walked erect in their own identities, look at him with envy and hatred for the poor security he enjoyed as a tenured employee of an institution that somehow could not fail. He did not give voice to this awareness; but the knowledge of common misery touched him and changed him in ways that were hidden deep from the public view, and a quiet sadness for the common plight was never far beneath any moment of his living."

To this point, the novel has focused persistently on personal tribulation. But Stoner has been conscious of the larger drama of class *the whole time*. These observations are not a footnote to the action, but a revelation of his worldview.

*

Does *Stoner* traffic in caricatures of the wealthy and the poor? Absolutely. Not all rich men are mendacious blowhards, nor are their daughters vapid viragos. The lives of all subsistence farmers are not "expended in cheerless labor, their wills broken, their intelligences numbed." That would be as absurd as, say, labeling impoverished African-American women "welfare queens."

But the portrayals of class in *Stoner* are about on par with what Dickens offers up in *A Christmas Carol*. Or Steinbeck in *The Grapes of Wrath*. Or, for that matter, what Jesus proclaims in the Sermon on the Mount. Which is to say that they are, by the standards of capitalism, heretical.

What I want to argue here is that *Stoner* is, in many ways, a far more radical social novel than works we commonly associate with that term. Because it suggests that the tolls of class cannot be overcome by individual action, that our inner lives are shaped by the economic injustice we experience, and witness, whether we ever say or do anything about it.

The social novels of the nineteenth century highlighted the transcendent power of personal resilience. Protagonists such as Jane Eyre and Pip are born low, but manage to scrap their way out of hardship. The thrill of these books is in seeing quality of character rewarded, both in romantic and economic terms. But there's always a certain genteel hedging. Yes, Jane Eyre marries her rich man in the end, but only after he's been mauled by fire and she's been bequeathed an inheritance.

The American social novels that preceded *Stoner* are far more explicit in addressing the systemic ills of class. Writers such as Sinclair Lewis, Willa Cather, Steinbeck, Jack London, and even Ernest Hemingway wrote books that dramatized the plight of modern capitalism. The *U.S.A. Trilogy* of John Dos Passos offers a sprawling account of men and woman trapped within a merciless caste system. The poor are invariably crushed while those who pursue wealth are dehumanized by greed.

Stoner is by no means a social novel in this tradition. Much of the reason it was overlooked back in 1965, when it was first published, is because critics were more focused on books that addressed the crises then roiling America, from civil rights to race riots. The private travails of a Midwestern academic, particularly one delivered in a reserved narrative style, came off as provincial, even stodgy.

But I've always thought of *Stoner* as a book that manages to fuse the themes of *The Great Gatsby* and *The Grapes of Wrath*. It shows us what happens when the poor farm boy actually gets the rich girl, which is that he winds up in hell. Not just because the rich girl is cruel and callow, but because she's been reared within a class system that programs her into passivity and egoism. Still worse, Stoner himself can never shed the stain of his poverty. His material circumstances improve. He's able to cultivate a vibrant intellect. But when it comes to his happiness, he cannot escape deprivation. *Stoner* is a fairytale in which the peasant boy becomes a man of means and lives sadly ever after.

*

It's no accident that my recent readings of this novel have gravitated toward issues of class. When I first read *Stoner*, I was barely thirty, single, and preoccupied by my artistic fate. If I was focused on politics, it was the personal morass of my graduate program.

But beginning with the election of 2000 and continuing through the atrocity of 9/11, I began to fret about the fragility of our democratic arrangement, a preoccupation that has infiltrated my work. I saw a cultural discourse increasingly driven by corporate hegemony and hostile to economic justice. The government that once launched a War on Poverty began, quite openly, to wage war on the poor.

Our most recent financial hemorrhage came as a result of Wall Street wizards packaging personal debt as assets, betting the house until the house went into foreclosure. Anyone with a functioning frontal lobe can see the seeds of the next great crash. It will again reside in our red ink, the credit cards we use to finance lives more extravagant than we can afford, the debits we accrue in pursuit of education and medical care in a society where the safety net has been meticulously unraveled and spun into gold for oligarchs.

But the depth of our delusions around wealth and poverty came into full view only a couple of years ago, when one of our major political parties nominated a candidate who had rehabbed his ruinous record as a businessman by portraying a gilded mogul on reality TV.

As a candidate, Trump offered little more than a showbiz spin on shopworn conservative cons; ginning up racial resentment, draping plutocratic aims in angry populism. But as a character in our psychic lives, Trump captivated us because he represented an ancient fantasy of wealth—that it confers boundless power, to lie with impunity, to massacre decency with a smirk.

To read *Stoner* in this age is to confront the true nature of faith in a capitalist theocracy: the rich succeed through virtue and industry, the poor fail because they are morally defective. These are the notions upon which we've staked the American story, the reason we've elected men who see public service as a means to consolidate wealth and power, protect privilege, and obliterate equal opportunity. No wonder our popular imagination has become consumed by outlaws who deploy gunshots as a shortcut to treasure. We've become a nation of wage slaves impatiently dreaming of bottle service, obedient to the dream.

On the campaign trail, our eventual president proclaimed, in all sincerity, "I love the poorly educated!" He knew his success required citizens to choose emotion over intellect, to become suspicious of those who learn too much, who study history or literature or science. The academic is no match for the entertainer in an attention economy. She can offer only the power to reflect, a power that steers us, inexorably, toward the hard truths of the inner life.

In this sense, Stoner is really just a front man, a farm kid who believes he will find refuge from the economic machinery of America in the life of the mind. The anguish he feels in witnessing men begging for bread isn't for the poverty of their circumstances, but for the shame stored up in their souls, a shame inflicted by those, like his in-laws, who live within the desolation of abundance.

We indulge in fantasies of wealth and power because we want to believe they will bestow us an ease of spirit, will undo the worry stamped upon us as children. But *Stoner* argues that there is no escape, even for a man like him who forges a life of economic security and spiritual meaning. He never escapes the deprivation of his youth. It merely assumes a new disguise in each phase of his life.

This about squares with my own experiences. From a financial standpoint, I've lived a life of extraordinary privilege.

And yet I remain persistently anxious about money, self-depriving—my wife might say miserly—and resentful of those who display the audacity to enjoy their wealth. Where does all this angst come from? My own lineage, which includes affluent bankers and card-carrying Communists, provides no coherent explanation. I can only speculate that I've been loyal to my parents, who worked hard and lived well below their means. And that I remain the child I was, who knew it was impossible to purchase happiness but hoarded his pennies anyway, just in case.

8. Monk Radical: Stoner as an Anti-War Novel

Precisely two sentences into the novel, we learn that William Stoner receives his PhD *at the height of World War I*. It's a subtle but telling detail, and Williams spends several pages describing the circumstances that lead to his decision.

Even before war is declared, and even within the ivied walls of the university, the tides of nationalism are surging. A number of students and younger instructors sign up as ambulance drivers for the allies and they are hailed as heroes. An anti-German fervor grips campus, leading to demonstrations "in which students shouted incoherently and waved American flags." A mob even confronts an aging German professor.

Stoner himself is precisely the kind of young man expected to enlist, which is to say poor and relatively powerless, reared with an obedience to authority, and therefore ripe for the instant heroism of soldiery. His friends Gordon Finch and Dave Masters both sign-up, and Finch—engorged with a sudden sense of his own purpose—cajoles Stoner to follow suit. "Gordon feels the first strength of virtue he's ever been allowed to feel," Masters explains, "and he naturally wants to include the rest of the world in it, so that he can keep on believing." This comment evokes the weeks and months after the terrorist attacks of 2001, when so many otherwise humane

Americans converted the rubble of a tragedy into a righteous pretext for vengeance.

For all his insight, Masters himself succumbs to cynicism. He confesses that he doesn't care about the moral stakes of the war, but that it might be "amusing to pass through the world once more" before retreating to the academy. It doesn't really matter whether he enlists or not, he reasons. Still, he urges Stoner to follow his example, not for God or country, but for himself. Trapped between this bewildering nihilism and Finch's self-aggrandizing fanaticism, Stoner is left no refuge.

But when he meets with Archer Sloane to announce his reluctant decision to enlist, the older man nearly lunges at him. To this point, Sloane has maintained a manner of courtly and ironic detachment toward his protégé. The contents of his heart now come pouring out.

He reveals that he has no memory of his own father, who was killed in the Battle of Shiloh. "A war doesn't merely kill off a few thousand or a few hundred thousand young men," he tells Stoner. "It kills off something in a people that can never be brought back. And if a people goes through enough wars, pretty soon all that's left is the brute, the creature that we— you and I and others like us—have brought up from the slime … the scholar should not be asked to destroy what he has aimed his life to build."

I didn't pay much attention to this passage in 1995. It may even have struck me as histrionic. But Sloane's words have taken on an entirely different valence in the America of 2019, a nation that has been at war for the past two decades, and that has witnessed, over that same span, a moral regression so profound that the brute now presides over our republic.

It's not just that work of academics and scientists has been cast aside. Our political leaders are now virtually indistinguishable from warlords. They traffic in racial incitement and fantasize about ethnic cleansing; they knowingly stoke the ire of domestic terrorists and embolden armed goon squads. They shrug when journalists are dismembered and liquefied in baths of acid. This is precisely what Sloane foresees. He understands that a population enthralled by martial heroism will inevitably devolve into a cult of violence whose only cause is an annihilating hatred.

*

Sloane eventually calms himself and counsels Stoner to remember who he is and what he has chosen to become. "There are wars and defeats and victories of the human race that are not military and that are not recorded in the annals of history," he explains.

As we know, Stoner is not in the habit of introspection. But he accepts the import of the verdict he must reach and sequesters himself in his room for two days. Over that span, he comes to realize that he's not frightened to join the fight, nor morally offended. What he feels is even more forbidden: a towering indifference. He simply cannot attach himself to the abstract mission of nationalism, or the atavistic ire that lies at the heart of patriotism. He realizes what he's known all along: that an unexpected passion for language rescued him from the deadness of agricultural servitude and that he has no interest in squandering that rebirth for the sake of a glory accorded by men more afraid of cowardice than moved by bravery.

Again: all this is happening in the earliest days of World War I. The entire population is ginned up on war. The Kaiser is being hung in effigy. Virtually every young man in his circle is enlisting, including his only two friends on earth. William Stoner chooses to heed the call of his inner life.

*

Gordon Finch immediately warns Stoner that he'll rue the decision. And as the war grinds on, Stoner does notice the contempt of older colleagues, and even students. But he doesn't care. He's simply unmoved by the public accounting of courage. Instead, as lists of the dead mount, Stoner begins to see mortality in a new way, not as a literary event or the body's slow surrender to illness but "the explosion of violence upon the battlefield, the gush of blood from the ruptured throat." A year into the war, word arrives that Dave Masters has been slain in France. The senselessness of this loss haunts Stoner for the rest of his life.

If Stoner remembers Masters as a defiant young man erased by war, Archer Sloane becomes a kind of dwindling shade. When Stoner meets with him to accept a full-time teaching position, he is shocked at Sloane's appearance. His eyes have gone dull, the skin of his face, "once tough as thin leather, now had the fragility of ancient, drying paper." It's like staring at a death mask.

On Armistice Day, the campus erupts and Stoner is caught up in a parade of students who sail past Sloane's office. Stoner returns to find his mentor weeping bitterly "at a defeat only he could see," the barbarism of celebrating a victory in which millions of human beings have been killed and dispossessed and traumatized for no purpose beyond the whim of the powerful. Sloane dies not long after.

Both of the men Stoner most admires in life are destroyed by war. Stoner thinks of Sloane two decades later, with the onset of World War II. He has come to understand, more fully, the truths that ravaged Sloane, "the futility of committing one's self wholly to the irrational and dark forces that impelled the world towards its unknown ends."

Williams began writing the novel in 1960, and sent a finished draft to his agent in 1963. The Vietnam War wouldn't begin for another two years, and there was no anti-war movement to speak of. I mention this to clarify that Williams wasn't motivated by his disgust at any particular war. Nor was he a pacifist. He served proudly in the Second World War, as a radio operator on transport planes in Burma. Three of his four published novels deal explicitly with masculine ambition and include scenes of extreme violence. His final book, unfinished at his death, was inspired by his war experiences.

Stoner is again the outlier. Its most persistent argument is that war represents, in every case, the harnessing of our inner life for the purpose of mass murder. There is no such thing as a good war, because the entire project disfigures the soul and dishonors the conscience.

To be clear, William Stoner has no political consciousness to speak of. He would never fight in a war, but it would never occur to him to protest one either. He is more like a monk who wishes only to be left alone in his abbey with his manuscripts. To him, literature is the purest expression of human enlightenment, the search for meaning and beauty. War is a desecration of that mission.

There is no shortage of novels in accord with this perspective. Many of Williams's own contemporaries, fellow veterans such as Mailer and Vonnegut and Heller, mined their military misadventures to craft famous anti-war novels. What sets *Stoner* apart is its refusal to place the drama of war at the center of human experience. In the world of the novel, war is something that happens elsewhere. But it is enabled by civilians who exalt the cause with no conception of its carnage.

Stoner predicts the moral disorder of our present, a world in which the sanctification of military endeavor is reflexive, while the horror of combat grows ever more abstract, in which airstrikes have become televised entertainment, in which the duty of service is peddled as a patriotic perk to the poor, in which young men are dispatched overseas to patrol villages with high-tech weapons, all to promote a set of interests that amount to a lucrative vendetta.

Archer Sloane sees it all coming. And he weeps.

9. Desire Shall Be Placed in Doubt

William Stoner is remarkably resilient in the face of hardship. But he's not impervious. At age forty-two, with his marriage and career in ruin, he reaches the end of his endurance. Unable to muster the attention necessary even to read, he sits for long periods, staring at nothing. He yearns for something, "even pain—to pierce him, to bring him alive."

In short, Stoner begins to wonder if his life is worth living. One snowy night, he turns out the lights in his office and listens to the silence, the sounds absorbed "by the delicate and intricately cellular being of the snow. Nothing moved upon the whiteness; it was a dead scene." He slips out of his own body and everything, from the trees to the pale planes of snow to the stars—appears tiny and far away, as if "dwindling to a nothingness."

This is the individual apprehended in a moment of pain so intense it triggers a cosmic disassociation. You don't have to be an English professor to hear the echoes here of Joyce ("his soul swooned slowly as he heard the snow falling faintly through the universe and faintly falling") and Frank O'Connor ("the old woman and the birds and the bloody stars were all far away, and I was somehow very small and very lonely"). But the passage has a more immediate echo; Stoner is encountering the ghost of his own parents, who spent their lives on the brink of being devoured by barren land.

I often point my students to this passage, as a demonstration of what I mean when I tell them to *slow down where it hurts*. I stress this because our tendency is to do just the opposite, to hurry past our most abject moments, as if by doing so we might erase them from the record of our inner life. Williams doesn't run from the darkness within Stoner. He runs into that darkness.

*

And yet.

And yet it's equally true that at this point in *Stoner*—we've hit page 180 of 278, folks—most readers are waiting for something good to happen to the guy. Not just waiting. Yearning. And Williams knows this. He understands the immutable logic of parable, in which the audience's hopes are inversely correlated to the hero's degree of tribulation.

Thus, as Stoner sits in his office staring suicidally at the shadows creeping across campus, he becomes aware of a figure standing behind him: Katherine Driscoll, the young instructor who showed such promise in his seminar.

Katherine asks Stoner to read a draft of her dissertation, explaining, quite nervously, that she revised her approach based on the class she took with him. He agrees. But he then spends a week ducking the task. Katherine hasn't just intruded upon his depression. She's asked him to feel alive again. When at last he sits down to read the draft (an hour before he's agreed to meet with her) its cogency startles him. He becomes so immersed that he misses their appointment and must drop by her apartment to find her. They talk for several hours. Stoner, we are told, leans so close "he could have extended his hand and touched her." But there is nothing leering in his regard for Katherine Driscoll. He's enthralled by her intellect and exhorts her to pursue the project, as Archer Sloane once did for him.

Katherine again mentions how vital his seminar was to her thinking. When he brushes off the compliment, she has one of those outbursts so common in *Stoner*, the sort that arise from feelings long concealed. It's shameful, she declares, how the class was turned against him.

He assures her the dispute is unimportant, and instantly recognizes the truth of his words. For the first time in months, he feels the weight of his depression lift. As he walks home, he notices a street light pushing "feebly against the darkness" and the smell of smoke from back yard fires "held by the mist." The world as a sensual experience comes alive again.

*

"And so he had his love affair."

We know this because Williams tells us so, even though the lovers in question will not consummate their desires for another six weeks. I note this to reiterate the singular pleasure of a narrative style in which the reader knows *more* than the characters.

The fact that William Stoner is a bit dense when it comes to his own motives, and slow to act on them, creates tremendous tension. Because the reader is constantly in a state of delayed gratification. We know what awaits Stoner, and because he doesn't we feel both curious and protective of him. I sometimes think of this as the Wile E. Coyote Principle.

Wile E. Coyote, for those of you not raised by a television, is a cartoon character who spends his life chasing the Roadrunner around the desert. From time to time, his enthusiasm sends him skittering off a cliff. Thanks to the wonders of animation, he will often stand suspended in the air for a few seconds before peering down and noticing his predicament, at which point gravity yanks him down. It is this moment of defiant ignorance that makes me love Wile E. Coyote, no doubt because I spend so much time in the same state.

When it comes to Katherine Driscoll, Williams has been dropping clues from the start—and making sure Stoner misses every one. The first time they talk, during the seminar, she blushes furiously and her eyes glint. He sees her "wreathed in radiant, secret, and intimate delight" and almost pulls back "from the sudden involuntary warmth."

After their initial discussion, Stoner begins to visit Katherine, always with the pretext of providing intellectual guidance. It's a form of courtship that mortifies Stoner. He thinks of himself as a "faintly ridiculous figure," a middle-aged man marooned in a miserable marriage, foisting himself upon a younger colleague. And yet he has to physically restrain himself from going to see her. Katherine feels the same countervailing passions. As they devote more energy to concealing their ardor, their encounters grow painfully awkward. Certain that his attentions have become an obligation, Stoner ceases visiting altogether.

A lovesick Katherine responds in kind: she stops showing up at school. Stoner hurries to her apartment, thinking her ill.

She must eventually clarify that she is not under the weather but desperately unhappy.

Stoner *still* doesn't get it.

Only after seeing her eyes "brilliant in pools of tears" does the truth land. At last, he confesses his feelings. Her reaction is a small masterpiece of understatement. "She did not move," Williams writes. "Two tears welled over her lashes and ran down her cheeks; she did not brush them away." Stoner prattles on, fumbling to explain his actions, until Katherine—speaking for all of us by now—tells him to shut up.

What follows is not a cinematic clinch but something much more familiar to those of us who recognize love as a force of profound disequilibrium. "Tentatively, clumsily, their hands went out to each other; they clasped each other in an awkward, strained embrace; and for a long time they sat together without moving, as if any movement might let escape from them the strange and terrible thing that they held between them in a single grasp."

*

No matter how often I read *Stoner*, I am always nearly breathless at this point, because Williams has so patiently constructed the ramp of desire. Both his lovers are delirious with wants their inhibitions forbid. And the reader is thus left to absorb all the ache. Which reminds me of something else I tell my students: *the most exciting thing about sex is desire.*

Which is not to say that the novel skimps on sex. William Stoner most definitely fucks. When he shows up at her place in the morning, they couple almost before they speak, on a bed "still rumpled and hot from Katherine's sleeping." After classes, they retreat to her apartment to make love, work on their books, then make love again.

So long denied the pleasures of the body, Stoner lets his "blunt fingers play upon the moist, faintly pink skin of thigh and belly" and lingers on the contours of her torso as well. Her flesh, we learn, has "a warm ruddy undertone like light flowing beneath a milky translucence. And like the translucent flesh, the calm and poise and reserve which he had thought were herself, masked a warmth and playfulness and humor whose intensity was made possible by the appearance that disguised them." Translation: Katherine is an angel in the streets and a devil in the sheets. Actually, the word she uses is more explicit: "Sometimes, with you, I feel like the slut of the world, the eager faithful slut of the world."

Well then.

As a reminder: all this is happening in the 1930s. In the Midwest. In the context of an extramarital affair between two professors of literature. But if there was one area Williams knew intimately, it was the academic affair.

For all the carnal abandon, the relationship is primarily one of tenderness. Stoner has lived through considerable strife. He possesses the nimble and curious mind of a scholar. But he is a fundamentally innocent person, one who has never experienced genuine intimacy. Consequently, he spends a lot of time simply trying to understand what love is.

This requires undoing some of the delusions he has acquired as a student of literature, the notion, for instance, that a life of the mind is at odds with a life of the senses. Katherine (no doubt speaking for Williams himself) flatly rejects this notion. She places her entire faith in "lust and learning." Stoner also frets that his infidelity will cause a marital crisis that jeopardizes his relationship to his daughter. Just the opposite happens. As he spends more time with Katherine, his relationship with Edith and Grace improves markedly.

Given the ruinous record of infidelity in literature, this twist might come off as a kind of wish fantasy for adulterers. In *Stoner*, the math works. Edith has long resented her husband's physical and emotional needs. The affair allows him fulfillment elsewhere, and alleviates the pressure on their loveless marriage. It also solidifies Edith's dominion over Grace. She begins to relax and her attitude toward Stoner softens into a kind of affection. For the first time in years, she allows him to spend time with Grace, and fixes up a spare bedroom for him. She also makes it clear that she knows about the affair and, to his astonishment, tacitly approves, so long as it doesn't threaten her security.

When Edith teases him about the youth of his paramour, Stoner briefly considers how others must see him, as a kind of desperate, wrinkled Lothario. But this caricature dissolves before his eyes.

Stoner is free. Not just to make love to Katherine, but to contemplate the meaning of love. The conclusion he reaches is one I have returned to again and again, in an effort to make sense of my own marriage, and my deepest friendships. As a child, Stoner conceives of love as an "absolute state of being" that one locates by good fortune. As a young man mired in a dead marriage, he dismisses it as "the heaven of a false religion." Only after meeting Katherine does he recognize that love is "neither a state of grace nor an illusion." He sees it as "a human act of becoming, a condition that was invented and modified moment by moment and day by day, by the will and the intelligence and the heart."

*

The author, having thus seduced us into shouldering the burden of hope, does what every great author must: he slowly strangles that hope.

The lovers are granted a blissful summer. In the fall, as campus fills up again, their affair becomes common knowledge. And yet no one seems to care. They begin to believe that they might be allowed to pursue their love, and with some dignity. Over the winter vacation, while Edith takes Grace to visit relatives, Stoner and Katherine head off to a cabin the Ozarks. They spend a week tromping through the snow, making love, laughing, and lying naked before a fire. It's a kind of idyll that provides a dreamy rejoinder to his nightmare honeymoon.

And if that's all there was to the novel, if it ended right there on page 206, I imagine most readers would set the book down with a dazed and grateful grin.

Alas, this is *Stoner*.

Gordon Finch calls Stoner to his office. Right on schedule, the novel delivers us to the intersection of astonishment and inevitability. "It's Lomax," Finch tells his old friend. "Somehow the son-of-a-bitch has got hold of it." His plan is to fire Katherine Driscoll on the basis of moral complaints made against her. The threat of a public hearing designed to sully her reputation will force Stoner to resign. If Stoner refuses, Lomax will publicly interrogate Katherine and he'll be dragged into the scandal, as if by accident.

*

Stoner staggers out of Finch's office and into the prison of the world. The single era of bliss in his life is over and a part of him feels "so near to death that he could watch the approach almost with calm." The dogwood trees are in bloom but they tremble "like soft clouds, translucent and tenuous" and the air is drenched with the "sweet scent of dying lilac blossoms." Stoner arrives at Katherine's apartment in a state of feverish gaiety, desperate to make her laugh, a laughter that is like "a dance that life makes upon the body of death." When at last he explains the situation, they quickly agree that they have no choice but to split up.

This isn't true. Stoner could resign and move elsewhere with Katherine. There would be a steep price: an acrimonious divorce from Edith, losing Grace, the anguish of the scandal. Stoner insists he's willing to bear all of it. But he can't abide the loss of their teaching careers, "the destruction of ourselves, of what we do."

I'm not sure I buy this, either. Even given the moral codes that prevailed in the 1930s, it seems plausible that Stoner would be able to find work as a professor eventually, or a headmaster. Katherine might have a harder time of it. But the idea that a divorce arising from infidelity would render them unfit to work as teachers of any kind in a city or town far from Columbus, Missouri, is pretty far-fetched.

Once again, Williams presents Stoner as a perfect martyr who has *no choice* but walk away from the love of his life. Every time I read this scene, Katherine's assent registers as both histrionic and avoidant ("I've known it all along, I guess ... But dammit all Bill! Dammit it all!") Within a few hours of their final doomed coupling, she submits her resignation and leaves town, an exit Stoner realizes she's been planning for some time.

It's all too convenient.

*

I say this because I can't stand to see Stoner throw away his only true shot at happiness. But I say it advisedly. I'm infected with a particular modern illness, the belief (perhaps it's a delusion) that human beings have a moral obligation to pursue joy, that the miraculous good fortune of finding a soulmate should transcend any other consideration, should compel us to absorb the risks of reinventing our lives. *Stoner* makes a different argument: that the preservation of selfhood inevitably requires the sacrifice of gratification.

I hate this idea. It makes me want to rip *Stoner* to shreds. Maybe it makes me want to rip the book to shreds because I fear it's true. But I don't think so. I see Stoner as a guy who's never forgiven himself for abandoning the family farm. He allows himself the ecstasy of loving Katherine. But only after decades of marital abuse, and only for a matter of months. Offered the chance to abandon a miserable marriage and job, he flinches, then attempts to recast his masochism as a moral imperative.

I didn't used to get so worked up about this, by the way. But the longer I've been alive, the more familiar I've become with the machinations of the inner life, the ways in which we sabotage our happiness by circling back to the sorrows of our youth. I've spent most of my adult life in pursuit of the feelings that dominated my childhood: loneliness, anxiety, humiliation. And that's before you get to the feuding.

But I've also spent a lot of time and money trying to undo this pattern, to overcome my hang-ups around happiness and success, to rid myself of the stubborn fiction that virtue resides in suffering.

It's not that William Stoner is making a disastrous decision here—that's true of virtually every character in the canon. It's that he regards his decision as saintly rather than self-punishing. Where, I always wonder, is the guy who celebrated love as a *human act of becoming*? The guy resurrected emotionally, erotically, even spiritually? How can that guy justify his decision to climb back into the crypt?

What a betrayal.

*

Williams was right about the nature of love. It is a process built by the will and the intelligence and the heart. I only wish that his novel offered a proving ground for that process, something more rigorous than an abject marriage or an ecstatic affair. Or that Stoner possessed the courage to live his creed. Most stories—maybe all of them, ultimately—arise from desire placed in doubt. But the fruition of desire generates its own vast and holy body of doubt. I know this from my own marriage. The true work of love resides in sticking with the process, especially in those moments, and eras, when desire is forced to coexist with doubt.

10. You're Going to Be a Teacher

One of the most enchanting scenes in *Stoner*—let's be honest here, it's a short list—is the meeting our hero has with Archer Sloane in the middle of his senior year. Sloane has summoned Stoner after noting the shift in his course of study from agriculture to English, a shift Stoner has concealed from his family and barely acknowledged to himself.

The official purpose of the meeting is to insure Stoner switches majors. But Sloane has a secret agenda. He asks the young man seated stiffly before him about his plans after graduation. In the grand tradition of clueless undergrads, Stoner has no idea what to say. The thought of returning to the family farm torments him. All he wants to do is immerse himself in literature. When Sloane suggests that he stay at the university to pursue an advanced degree, Stoner can scarcely conceive of such a possibility. Sloane is left with no choice but to bomb another truth bomb on his protégé.

"'But don't you know, Mr. Stoner,' Sloane asked. 'Don't you understand about yourself yet? You're going to be a teacher.'"

This pronouncement triggers a familiar sensation within Stoner: his world disjoints. Sloane floats off into the distance. The walls of the office recede. Stoner himself feels as if he's suspended in midair. He dazedly asks Sloane if he's sure.

"It's love, Mr. Stoner," Sloane says cheerfully. "You are in love. It's as simple as that."

*

Remarkably, amid a life in which every other form of love invites disaster, it is *as* simple as that.

Stoner is not much of a teacher at first. He's too aware of the gap between his own enthusiasm and his capacity to inspire his students. But gradually he sheds his inhibitions and becomes so immersed in his lectures that he forgets all about himself and his doubts.

Stoner is embarrassed by these outbursts, but they enthrall his students, and their papers begin to show signs of emotion and imagination. He has begun to transmit to them his love of literature, a love "which he had hidden as if it were illicit and dangerous" and which he displays, "tentatively at first, and then boldly, and then proudly."

I adore this formulation of teaching, that it begins at the precise moment when passion overpowers self-consciousness. The teacher reveals his inner life and this revelation elicits a mimetic response in his students. It's no accident that religion is nearly absent in William Stoner's life. His faith emerges in the classroom; his calling is the fragile process of drawing students out of themselves.

He clings to the lovely and childish belief that the academy prizes this calling above all else and he sacrifices everything (love, happiness, his health) for the privilege of teaching. Here is the entirety of the speech he delivers at his retirement party: "I do not know what I would have done if

I had not been a teacher. I want to thank you all for letting me teach."

*

Every great teacher I've met shares this overweening devotion. They arrive in our lives like some variety of lodestar, dispatched to steer us to an unforeseen fate. If that sounds hokey, please take a quick spin through your own life and note how many teachers figure in your pantheon of personal heroes.

I can still remember every teacher I had in grade school, their faces, their gestures, their aromas. (My third-grade teacher, Rosalie Shepard, would be happy to know that my youngest daughter is her namesake.) I became a writer because Mr. Farrell, my ninth-grade English teacher, blew my head off by reading us the opening chapter of *Catcher in the Rye*, swear words and all. I worked up the courage to leave journalism because John DuFresne, an actual literary writer, allowed me to attend a weekly workshop he held Friday afternoons, something he did for free, on top of his duties as a father and full-time professor.

I even remember teachers I didn't like much at the time, the dyspeptic Monsieur Weiss, for instance, whose giant nose was a blasted volcano of purple capillaries and whose French lessons inevitably devolved into ranting against our lassitude. He wore a beret and cable-knit cardigans and it broke his heart that we didn't share his amour for *la belle langue*. That's what I can't shake, I guess: how much he cared.

I can already see the teachers my own kids will never

forget, the ones with that indelible capacity to elicit love: Deb Jacobs, who guided all three through nursery school (and kept us from freaking out), Ms. Fassel, who taught Jude to knit, Mrs. Jette, who inspired Josie to become a feminist, and the indomitable Dr. Lambert, who has brought science alive for her. They are all excessively generous. Like old Archer Sloane they are all saying, in their own manner: *Don't you see? It's love!*

*

At the same time, it's important to recognize that Stoner's relationship with Archer Sloane is exceptional. Sloane is not the kind of guy who marches around sprinkling the fairy dust of literary curiosity onto unsuspecting sophomores. To most of his students, he's a hard-ass who eventually becomes an embittered hard-ass.

Stoner celebrates what teaching can be, in other words, without idealizing the process. Despite his dedication, William Stoner is often ineffective. He understands that the essential currency of teaching—attention to the material being taught, to students, and to their work—doesn't always yield learning; pupils must feed their own attention into the system. He teaches most effectively in the years after World War II, when a new breed of student begins to appear in his classes, veterans who are "contemptuous of triviality" and approach their studies "as if those studies were life itself and not a specific means to specific ends."

All of which is to say that the particular relationship between a student and teacher has much to do with luck, how and when they encounter one another, the ghosts they carry.

I should reiterate here that my initial reading of *Stoner* coincided with my return to the academy. If I'm honest, the vision of teaching it offered no doubt inflated my expectations. I dreamed of being taught by Sloanes, not Lomaxes.

Of course, Professor X did play the role of benevolent guide to any number of students. He just happened to find me disrespectful, and perhaps threatening. I suspect some of his contempt for me arose from the disappointment I expressed in him, which in turn arose from me holding him to an impossible standard, which in turn arose from reading a novel that only reached me because of his passionate advocacy. Life is strange.

*

I did learn a lot about teaching from the workshops in grad school, though most of the lessons were rather dark. I saw what happens when teachers are dismissive of student work, and critical of other professional writers, which is that students ape these behaviors. I learned that some teachers run workshops as Darwinian filters, weeding out the weak. Maybe that works. There's a whole crowd out there that views MFA culture as too coddling, a bastion of mediocrity and therapeutic groupthink. But I hated being in those workshops. It was like revisiting my youth: a room full of needy siblings, with a dad content to watch them wail on each other.

I became a teacher, in part, to revise my own childhood. But I also wanted to hand out a few revelations of my own. That's why most writers wind up teaching: because at some point we've fallen in love with literature—"the mystery of the mind and heart showing themselves in the minute, strange, and unexpected combinations of letters and words"—and we're itching to share the good news. It's an evangelical compulsion.

I was naïve enough to assume that I was making a sound financial decision, too. (Those of you who teach for a living can stop laughing at some point.) I moved to Boston, a few years before the millennium rolled, fully intending to support myself by teaching. Being an actual professor at an actual university struck me as a prestigious arrangement, one that would underwrite my inevitable literary ascent.

I had yet to encounter the Adjunct Racket, the manner in which higher education had been refashioned into a for-profit industry during the Reagan Revolution. The folks in accounting had cut costs by shifting class loads from tenured professors to part-timers who required no institutional support. I spent several years careening between three different universities, in a mint green Toyota Tercel whose rusted undercarriage would eventually surrender its front left tire to the Fresh Pond Parkway.

Like every other adjunct in the city—and there were a lot of us, stashed away in our septic garrets, pecking away at our glorious hopeless manuscripts—I taught mostly freshman composition. I was not a very good teacher, because I didn't know or care what freshman composition actually was; I guessed it had something to do with theme essays. I also lacked the patience and/or executive function required to prepare class plans. Remembering the code to three different Xerox machines was about all I could handle.

I should have been reading books about rhetoric and the building blocks of composition, books with titles like *How to*

Assign and Assess Theme Essays Without Dying of Grief. But I was busy reading *Stoner* for the thirteenth time, waiting for my big Stoner moment. I scanned my classes for big-knuckled farm boys. But it was just the usual rabble of suburban Catholics (Boston College) and closeted goths (Emerson) and they didn't want to be there either.

I tried to get by on charm, which is tricky when your charm is comprised of profanity and unfortunate facial hair. My pedagogy in those days consisted of forcing students to read my favorite short stories, then forcing them to listen to me talk about my favorite short stories. I had passion. I was *trying* to transmit. But my narcissism suffocated those rooms. It crushed curiosity.

I did better when I snagged a creative writing class, or was allowed by some negligent overlord to design a class of my own. I still remember the buzz of reading particular student stories in which the writers—many of them as shy and uncertain as Stoner himself—suddenly discovered language as an instrument of truth. Jesus. Those stories! Those fearless, rhythm-drunk sentences! It was as if their souls had exploded onto the page. I still don't know how they did it. But it had something to do with what Stoner describes, that act of contagious disinhibition, of persuading them out of themselves.

Sometimes I pulled an Archer Sloane and put the touch directly on a student. Tracy Wigfield showed up in my course on cultural criticism. Like many Boston College students, she looked as if she'd stepped out of J. Crew catalogue. But I could see her taking everything in, the Didion, the Ephron, the Foster Wallace. Her comments were so deadpan that other students would cock their heads.

During office hours I told her what she already knew: that she should stop being so obedient and let some of her subversive wit onto the page. The next piece she brought to class was a teleplay for a press conference delivered by Barbie (the doll), a savagely droll piece that I immediately read to my wife, whose sole comment was this: "She's funnier than you." A few years later, I received an embossed card from Tracy thanking me for my encouragement and informing me that she was now the head writer on a television show called *30 Rock*. Had I heard of it? I was proud beyond measure while also wanting to hang myself.

*

This is not to say that I was batting 1000 percent, or even .250. For every Tracy Wigfield there were a dozen students who did just enough to earn a grade-inflated B, and one or two with enough discernment to recognize their disinterest as my doing. They would scorch me on the student evals, which I used to post around my apartment in an effort to appear hip and self-effacing. *If writing were a part of my body I would cut it off with an exacto blade.* That was one of my favorites.

When I finally nabbed a graduate fiction workshop—a coup in the adjunct racket—I botched it. I allowed a charismatic and aggrieved student to poison the class. I should have had the courage to meet with her privately. But I wanted to avoid the conflict, to win her over, so I let her sit there scowling, and every week I grew more rattled, less certain I had anything to say.

I've gradually figured out how to deal with such students. I taught an MFA workshop on memoir a few years back. The second week, the dean summoned me to a meeting. A student had filed a complaint against me, objecting to my having assigned an essay by Cheryl Strayed that used the word "slut." I was handed a massive binder labeled *Sensitivity Training*, and urged to issue a proviso before distributing such potentially upsetting selections, affirming that the views and language deployed were those of the writer, and not me, the professor.

"Isn't that what the byline is for?" I asked.

When I arrived for the next class, the woman who had filed the complaint was seated in my chair. She glanced at me triumphantly—my own Charles Walker.

I got it. She didn't like me. She didn't like that a man was teaching a class full of female students. I didn't blame her. I didn't like it either. But I also understood that she was trying to draw me into a conflict, one that would derail the class. I didn't take it personally. I didn't react at all. I was more interested in her writing than her agenda.

My point is that students are going to work through their issues with you. Like it or not, you're a transference figure. That's why Williams spends so much time in Stoner focused on the relationships that develop between students and teachers. The entire plot of the second half of the novel arises from the dynamics within a single seminar, in which one student plots against Stoner while another falls in love with him.

That's a rather extreme set of student issues to work through. But every teacher must do two jobs at once in the classroom: stimulate the intellect while managing the emotions. In my own teaching, which involves personal creative work, the two are inseparable. Every time I walk into a workshop my goal is to create a community trusting enough that its members can be completely honest with one another, both in their writing and in their feedback.

That takes work. The teacher has to take everyone in the room seriously, has to pay attention at all times, and has to make it clear—both explicitly and implicitly—that all the petty bullshit we lug around gets checked at the door. For Stoner, a teacher is "simply a man to whom his book is true, to whom is given a dignity of art that has little to do with his foolishness or weakness or inadequacy as a man." Great teachers are able to inspire this self-belief, so that their students become more assured in their own knowledge and talent while also becoming humbler, more full of wonder at all they don't yet know or understand.

*

The sort of teaching I do sits at the apex of privilege. Like Stoner, I get to work with students who view writing *as life itself and not a specific means to specific ends*. It's easy to reach those who arrive eager to be transformed.

But just imagine the teachers who walk into crumbling classrooms to find thirty-seven restive kids, most of whom experience the educational process as little more than elaborate warehousing scheme. Third-grade teachers in the public schools of Liberty City or East St. Louis or El Paso have an almost unimaginable burden. Forget igniting the sacred flame of learning; they've got to make sure nothing gets burned down. They have to shift, from moment to moment, between being educators, social workers, prison guards, and surrogate parents. They have to run a continual triage on the forgotten children of this country, marshaling their internal reserves, figuring out which students are worth saving, or trying to save.

It may appear that I've veered off the path here, but remember that Stoner is, at root, the story of a child forgotten by society, a boy destined for a life of manual labor, who finds a path to prosperity and meaning in learning.

I can't for the life of me figure out why the key figures in our educational system—teachers in such settings—are not more widely revered and rewarded. In any morally sane society, they would be paid a CEO's salary. And CEOs would be forced to drive used Honda Civics and buy their own fucking office supplies.

I don't mean to suggest that every teacher is a saint. But anyone who believes that people go into teaching for the job security, or because it sounds like a great way to get summers off, hasn't spent much time in an actual school. Teachers become teachers, and stay teachers, because they believe in the holy process of transmission.

*

I now work for a foundation where I get to teach American and foreign-born journalists, most of whom have reached the top of their field through decades of diligence. My class offers them the chance to write creative non-fiction, pieces that are more intimate and reflective than the stories they produce for large media companies.

Just a few weeks ago, we workshopped an essay by a woman who wrote a candid account of the cruelty within her family. Her colleagues spent a good deal of time praising this candor and marveling at her descriptive powers. Then, toward the end of class, a man I'll call Kaito spoke up.

Kaito is a Japanese reporter who covers business for a large news service. He's a quiet, earnest guy (not unlike Stoner really) who escaped his small town by focusing doggedly on professional advancement. Though he has been writing in a second language, and in an entirely new way, Kaito has become transfixed by the process. His essay for class was about his brother, and he told me, somewhat bemusedly, that he couldn't stop working on it. He had to write every day; his wife was starting to complain. He critiqued his classmates in the same compulsive manner, often reading their pieces several times over the course of a few days, then marking them up.

Kaito told the woman in question that he had adored her essay, that her prose was nearly flawless. Then he paused for a long moment and furrowed his brow. "There is a lot of anger in the piece toward your family," he said softly. "I see the reasons why. But what I must say to you now—and I hope you forgive me for being so direct—is that this piece is not the whole truth yet." He looked at the writer tenderly. "Because I have come to know you as a person. I know how much love there is in you. I have seen it. This love is there for your family, too. Not just what is on the page."

It was one of the most transcendent moments I've experienced as a teacher. The writer could feel the truth of what he'd said, that she was using rage to conceal her woe. We all felt it.

I ran into Kaito before our next class, and thanked him for having spoken so movingly. He tipped his face down a little, as he often does. "I had to do it," he said. "That's our job. We can't allow a colleague to fall short of the truth in their work." I could tell right then—I'd known it for some time already, I guess—that Kaito was a teacher.

Don't you see? I wanted to shout out. *It's love!*

11. Lessons in Helplessness

In the past few years, I've been thinking about an aspect of *Stoner* I barely noticed as a younger man: fatherhood. This has to do with my own struggles as a dad, which I'll come to after some artless stalling.

For now, let's recall that Grace comes into Stoner's life as an unexpected blessing, after Edith essentially vanishes. During the first year of her life, the child knows "only her father's touch, and his voice, and his love." Grace winds up spending hours in her father's study, working alongside him at a little desk. She is a quiet and thoughtful child, and the two of them share a kinship Stoner recognizes as central to his existence—until the evening Edith appears in the doorway, determined to evict Grace.

It's important to note the fluctuations in this scene. Edith orders Grace out. Stoner insists she's no bother. Edith ignores him and repeats her directive. Bewildered, Grace rises from her chair and walks toward the door. She then pauses in the center of the room, "looking first at her father and then at her mother." Grace is just trying to figure out who's in charge, of course. But she's also, by my reckoning, imploring her father to rescue her.

When you examine the situation from her perspective,

you can see why. Stoner isn't just a doting father. He has been, to this point, her protector, shielding her from a mother who is domineering and destructive. This is why Stoner's response always lances my heart: "*'It's all right, Grace,' he said as gently as he could. 'It's all right. Go with your mother.'*"

It's not all right. He's sending her soul off to an execution.

*

I wish I were overstating this. Williams leaves no room for doubt. Edith immediately overhauls Grace's life in a manner inimical to her nature. She dresses her up like a doll and forces her to host parties and enlists her in piano lessons. She hovers and controls (as her own mother did) without any expression of love. Stoner can't quite admit to himself the horror of what's happening. But Grace knows. One day, he encounters her in the living room. They exchange shy smiles and Stoner kneels to embrace his daughter. Her body stiffens. She's become a hostage.

In the midst of this hug, Grace's face again registers *bewilderment*, a word repeated to emphasize the mystery with which this little girl is contending: she doesn't understand why her father isn't trying to protect her.

Stoner does finally confront his wife, imploring her not to "use the child" to punish him. Given their history, we understand why Stoner feels attacked. But Edith's primary motive has nothing to do with him. She's trying to rescue herself from a life without purpose or companionship. Grace has never been happier, she insists. Stoner is taken aback by the scale of his wife's delusion but lacks the strength to impose his will.

Grace eventually retreats into despondence. When Edith tries to browbeat her into sociability, the girl responds by growing fat, "as if something inside her had gone loose and soft and hopeless." Stoner knows, and has long known, that Grace is "one of those rare and always lovely humans whose moral nature was so delicate that it must be nourished and cared for." Though "avid for tenderness and quiet" she is left to endure "indifference and callousness and noise." Stoner sees all this. But there's a world of pain between seeing and doing, as the novel reminds us over and over.

Stoner chooses instead to regard the emotional abuse of his daughter as a fait accompli. "He did not allow himself the easy luxury of guilt," Williams writes. "Given his own nature and the circumstance of his life with Edith, there was nothing that he could have done. And that knowledge intensified his sadness as no guilt could have, and made his love for his daughter more searching and more deep."

*

I honestly have no idea what this is supposed to mean. I *think* Williams means that Stoner is so inherently passive, and Edith so obstinate, that there is nothing he can do to defend Grace. Any effort he might summon will trigger his wife's hysteria and further damage his daughter. But honestly: how much worse can things get for Grace? She's presented as utterly broken in spirit.

Let us imagine, for a moment, the betrayal Grace must be experiencing. The father whose adoration was the central condition of her life has abandoned her to the whim of a disturbed mother. Even if Stoner can't rescue his daughter, shouldn't he try? Isn't that what Grace yearns to see, that she matters at least that much? Because otherwise, what message is she receiving from her father?

I would argue that the helplessness Grace exhibits throughout her life is learned directly from her father, who insists that this helplessness intensifies his love. But what good is love if it remains inert and invisible to its recipient? What good is a father who functions only as a passive witness to his child's suffering? And if we're really going to parse this passage—as it appears we're going to—since when is guilt an easy luxury? That sounds like the kind of sentiment endorsed by someone who's trying to avoid feeling guilty.

But shouldn't Stoner feel guilty about his abdication here? This isn't a matter of his own suffering, or that of another adult, such as Katherine. This is his child we're talking about.

*

As a teenager, Grace grows into beauty and popularity, which pleases her mother, who has no idea that this popularity arises from her promiscuity. Stoner makes one final effort to advocate on his daughter's behalf, urging her to move away for college. Edith, who previously signed off on the plan, suddenly implores "Gracie" not to leave her "mommy" all alone. Grace looks at her mother then turns "very briefly to her father" and shakes her head.

Stoner tries to intervene, but Grace won't look at him again. "It doesn't matter," she replies. That's her verdict on the matter. The acquiescence here isn't just obedience to an overbearing mother. It's the inevitable response to a father who has failed to advocate for her, or himself.

Grace does find a way to escape her home: she gets pregnant, the result of a drunken tryst her first year in college. Edith orchestrates a hasty marriage of convenience. Stoner gazes upon the bride and thinks of the girl who once kept him company and "looked at him with solemn delight, as a lovely child who long ago had died."

Grace moves to St. Louis with her new husband, who ships off to World War II, where he is promptly killed. She gives birth to a son but refuses to return to Columbia. Rather than embracing motherhood, Grace surrenders the care of her child to her in-laws. It might be said that she is repudiating her mother's catastrophically controlling behavior, or that she's reenacting her father's negligence. The truth is probably somewhere in between.

What becomes apparent during her rare visits home is that Grace copes with her life by drinking. Watching her hopeless descent into alcoholism, Stoner feels a sense of loss he can "scarcely bear." He can see the dimensions of her future, that she will continue to drink, more and more each year, "numbing herself against the nothingness her life had become. He was glad she had that, at least; he was grateful that she could drink."

I know what Stoner means. But it's a damning indictment of him as a parent, ultimately, a feeble acknowledgment that his own daughter has been reduced to a slow suicide.

*

It may come as a surprise that Grace appears on only a handful of pages. Fatherhood is a harrowing but peripheral aspect of *Stoner*, perhaps because fatherhood was a peripheral aspect of John Williams's life. Like most of his male contemporaries (Bellow, Updike, Mailer, et al) his energies were devoted to more worldly ambitions.

In the same way he created an idealized love affair with Katherine—hot, soul-nourishing, and undone by a cruel meddler—Williams portrays Stoner's paternal instincts as impeccable. If not for Edith, we are left to presume that Stoner would have guided Grace into a happy and actualized adulthood. It's a vision of unrequited fatherhood devised by a man who chose not to spend much time with his kids.

But the portrayal of family in *Stoner*, however extreme, captures a couple of indelible truths. First, that troubled people tend to be the most powerful figures in a family, the most effective at exporting their internal discord into the world around them. Second, that inaction, especially by parents, often matters more than misguided action.

In the stories I tell about growing up, the central feature usually isn't the tyranny of my parents but their absence, and the resulting bedlam. Then again, families are complex systems. My parents have pointed out, rather reasonably, that at a certain point they could no longer contain the dark energies I and my brothers generated.

I'm thinking here of an episode that took place during high school. I had taken our dog out for a walk after dinner and when I returned home I saw my twin brother Mike brandishing a butcher knife in the manner of a slasher movie villain.

He had stationed himself outside the door to our garage and was bellowing homicidal threats at our older brother, Dave, who was locked inside. I had missed the first act of this play, which took place at the dinner table and culminated with Dave plunging a fork into Mike's thigh.

What I remember most vividly from this episode was my mother's face, floating behind the window pane beside our front door. Her expression was one of utter helplessness. It wasn't just that my brothers were too physically strong for her to control. It was the intensity of their hatred, which was by then beyond the reach of maternal love.

*

Stoner presents a family in which a broken mother and a submissive father undermine their daughter. Grace becomes human wreckage. I recognized the tragedy of her fate before I had kids. But I never got riled up about it. I never turned on Stoner. And I never broke down at the vision of her drunken surrender, as I do now.

The arrival of my three children has brought immense joy to my life, which is what every parent says right before they confess to how exhausting and exasperating and tedious their kids are. In fact, those are the easy emotions, the punchlines. It's much harder to talk about how responsible we feel as parents, and how terrified.

Because we were often lonely and frightened during our own childhoods, Erin and I tend to fixate on the happiness of our kids. We're more identified with them, more protective of them, more vulnerable to their moods.

This has been especially true of Rosalie, our youngest. She's the sort of kid who registers as impervious. At age five, she does a lot of yelling and not much listening. Her mind gallops. She can be inconsiderate, even vicious, without much apparent remorse. Every week or so, she steps on someone's last nerve and that someone, usually me, yells at her. At which point she crumbles. "Everybody hates me!" she'll wail. "Everybody wants me to die."

What's gutting about such moments is the sudden revelation of her fragility. Beneath all the bluster is a little girl overmatched by the world of giants around her, painfully aware of the frustration she generates, and scared she'll be abandoned. I do what any parent would. I whisper an apology for losing my patience. I set my lips to her burning brow. I pledge my love. And yet I can't help but feel that I've failed her somehow.

This is how it works with kids. They don't do subterfuge. One way or another, they tell you the truth. The only question is whether you can bear to hear it.

I still remember the tantrum our son Jude threw after his uncle's wedding. Erin and I were at odds, the ceremony had everybody stressed out, and Jude, at age three, had absorbed these dark valences. He was so inconsolable that I eventually had to carry him upstairs to a little apartment above the reception area. "I want you to help me come down, Papa!" He kept howling these words at me.

I told him I couldn't bring him downstairs because he was too upset.

"I want you to help me come down! Help me come down, Papa!"

On and on it went until, to my horror, I picked him up

and threw him onto a couch. "You're not going anywhere until you calm down, you little shit!" I thundered. My son looked at me. He was frightened, but also genuinely mystified. And instantly, I realized what he was actually saying to me, what he had been saying for the past half an hour: *I want you to help me calm down, Papa.*

He'd been pleading with me to soothe him, to tame the panic that had taken possession of his body. And what had I done? Hurled him onto a couch.

*

The point isn't that I'm a shitty dad. The point is that being a dad means dealing with the shitty parts. *Stoner* presents a vision of fatherhood that is virtually shit-free. Stoner is either perfectly attuned to his daughter, or ruthlessly torn from her. I get that domestic norms in the 1930s called for mothers to oversee child rearing. But that doesn't absolve Stoner. Given what he sees happening to Grace, he has a duty to try.

What's more, the longer I've been a father the more I've come to feel that this duty is something closer to an honor. The opportunity to comfort your child in a grueling moment, to offer succor, however imperfectly, is sacred and fleeting. Because the influence you wield over your kids starts diminishing the moment they can crawl away from you.

I've been wrestling with this unwelcome realization over the past year, as my eldest, Josie, enters the rough sea of adolescence. I can see that she's worried and sad, as I was at her age, and that she wants me to know this and, at the same time, that she wants to hide every trace of her suffering from me. As I've struggled to figure out how to help her, my mind keeps doubling back to the description of Grace from Stoner: *she was one of those rare and always lovely humans whose moral nature is so delicate that it must be nourished that it might be fulfilled.*

I find myself thinking about her first few weeks of life. Josie had trouble breastfeeding, so she suckled formula from a tiny surgical tube I taped to my finger. While Erin slept down the hall, the two of us sat in a cradle of darkness. It was a hushed and lovely scene, but one steeped in panic. I was frantic to get calories into her. Some irrational part of me looks back at this tableau and sees the anguish of my inner life seeping from my body into hers.

For years, we saw Josie as an ebullient kid, prone to worry but mostly unshadowed by shame. As her body contends with womanhood, she's become withdrawn, even defiant, the watchful guardian of new and veiled sorrows. I'd spoken with enough parents of teenagers to know we'd reach this point. And yet, as with every other parent on earth, I never quite believed it would happen to me.

The perfect dad would be sensitive and measured in responding to Josie, would recognize her provocations as manifestations of her pain. But there is no perfect dad. He doesn't exist. When Josie pushes me away, I push back. I badger her to open up, and retreat into petulance when she refuses. I've blown up at her. I've stood outside her locked door, knowing I've fucked up, that I've scared her, panting with shame. In such moments, I fear I've lost my daughter forever, that we'll never find our way back to the trust and ease we enjoyed early in her life.

And this is why *Stoner* has become a different book for me, a book about the loss of a beloved daughter, about the rupture of a special bond and the slow torture of watching a child retreat from your love.

If I'm furious at William Stoner for not doing more to protect his daughter, as I clearly am, it's mostly because I want to indulge in the fantasy that a sufficiently loving parent can save his child from the grasp of despair. It's bullshit, and I know it's bullshit. I know it from my family of origin. My parents did all they could to recognize our struggles and get us help; they still had to watch us battered by depression and bouts of self-destruction, midnight visits to the ER and worse.

When Josie was about six months old, we threw a naming party for her. What I remember most vividly is the talk I had toward the end of the evening with an older couple. They were both therapists, gentle souls. Josie was crawling nearby in her blue velvet dress. The mother gazed at her for a long moment, her eyes gleaming. Then she was weeping, silently, and her husband put his arm around her and murmured that their eldest daughter was living in New York City and was in trouble with drugs and they were completely wrecked.

"It goes so fast," the mother said. That was all she could get out.

*

I realize this is all sounding rather abject. I don't mean it to. There's a great deal of laughter and cuddling in our home. The kids are relentless creators. They make drawings and songs and rocket ships. They read for hours. They're beloved by teachers and friends. This is what I try to hold onto: their kindness, their bustling imaginations. That's hard to do, though, when you're worried sick.

I might condemn William Stoner for his dereliction and his rationalizations, but in the end, he is merely the standard bearer of a helplessness that afflicts every parent. To raise a child is to confront the limits of your power over the inner life of another, even a treasured child. There are no heroes in this club, only survivors.

My own lessons in helplessness have just begun. They'll stack up around me as my children pass into the world and shape their own fates, hand their hearts to the wrong people, suffer the arrows of outrageous fortune, chase their hopes into unseen hazards. To become themselves, our children will have to outgrow the people we imagine them to be, the ones we can keep safe. What I mean (without especially wanting to) is that every parent winds up gazing backward—like Stoner, like that weeping mother—at a lovely child who died long ago.

12. Death Becomes You

In the Spring of 1949, William Stoner receives a circular in the mail announcing the publication of a book by Katherine Driscoll, who is teaching at a good liberal arts college in Massachusetts and remains unmarried. That same day, Stoner resigns his position at the university, calmly tells Edith that he is leaving her the house and all its possessions, and travels east by train, where he is reunited with Katherine. He finds a position at a college near hers and they spend their remaining years learning and loving in a cozy cape bungalow.

Kidding!

This is *Stoner*, people. You get perfect martyrdom, not actualization.

Instead, Stoner immediately orders the book, all the better to flog himself. As he reads the dedication (*To W.S.*) his eyes blur and he sits "for a long time without moving." You will have noticed by now that Williams does this a lot; he shows us Stoner lodged, paralyzed really, in a moment of affliction. Because he has invariably set out the precise cause and nature of this affliction there is no need to elaborate. It's enough for us to have to sit with the guy, knowing all we do, and to feel what he feels. Which is, of course, our own particular version of his pain.

I want to emphasize this because so often writers believe—are encouraged in this belief by agents and editors and the like—they have to show characters doing things, making their emotions manifest, taking action. But a person trapped in stillness, thinking and feeling deeply—is action. The action of the inner life.

Stoner reads the rest of Katherine's book in one sitting. In the passion and clarity of her prose, in the literary fervor that fueled their courtship, Katherine comes alive again. It's as if she's in the next room. Stoner's hands begin to tingle. A sense of loss engulfs him. At nearly sixty, Stoner thinks, he should be beyond the force of such passion. But he's not beyond his passion, and he knows in this moment that he never will be.

Archer Sloane may have been the first person to recognize the churning heart beneath his stillness. But Stoner has given his passion instinctively, first to literature, then to Edith, and later Katherine. "He had, in odd ways, given it to every moment of his life, and had perhaps given it most fully when he was unaware of his giving," Williams writes. "It was a passion neither of the mind nor of the flesh; rather, it was a force that comprehended them both, as if they were but the matter of love, its specific substance. To a woman or to a poem, it said simply: Look! I am alive."

This is the ocean that roils within all of us, that will not relent, nor be subdued by our mightiest suppressive efforts. We cannot stop paying attention to the world, seeking attention from it, and because attention is the first and final act of love, we cannot stop loving.

*

How enchanting to land on that last line. *Look! I am alive.* It always makes me feel like I'm going to live forever. And I think Williams knew this. Because it is at this point in the novel that he begins to lower the boom. And by boom, I mean mortality. Within a few pages, Stoner is listening to a young pink-faced doctor who informs him, hesitantly, that there is a giant tumor in his intestines, which they need to remove as soon as possible. The last twenty pages of the novel are devoted to a tender and meticulous accounting of Stoner's death.

This may sound like a dismal way to end the story. But it may be the most radical decision Williams makes. As Americans, we spend an expanding share of our psychic and material reserves railing against mortality, trying to prolong the journey, rendering death a villainous interloper, rather than the natural culmination visited upon every living creature. There's a lot of money to be made from terror, of course, so the industrialization of death denial is inevitable in a society struggling to feel alive and deranged by greed.

But I'm equally fascinated by the mask death wears in popular culture. Our screens are awash with corpses, nearly all of them the product of some traumatic criminal event. Half the dramas on basic cable involve sexy forensics sleuths. All they care about is how the living got dead. You barely ever see any consideration of those bodies that die slowly, unheroically, of the physical deterioration wrought by disease, and, in particular, of the restless mind within that expiring flesh.

This remains a mystery, even within our literature: what do the dying think about? How do they reckon with their past, with what's happening to them, with the end of their existence? The inner life of death. That's the last province *Stoner* visits.

*

You've already figured out that Stoner isn't going to make it easy for himself. Indeed, for a hardcore masochist, a serious and undetected cancer is just what the doctor ordered. Stoner keeps his illness a secret naturally. This isn't forbearance, or denial. It's a kind guardianship. He knows he doesn't have much time and he's not ready to have his attention distracted by the drama of dying.

Fresh off the fatal diagnosis, he pauses to take in a set of stairs he's traversed thousands of times but never really seen. "The steps were marble," Williams notes, "and in their precise centers were gentle troughs worn smooth by decades of footsteps." Stoner thinks of "time and its gentle flowing" and suddenly the stone is transformed into a relic of the living, the solid made liquid, the inanimate made mortal. I love that about the guy. He never stops paying attention.

Stoner has been engaged in this dance between the physical and metaphysical worlds his entire life; the prospect of dying creates a new urgency. But he has worldly tasks to complete before he can attend to the question of his own meaning. Lomax has been clamoring for him to retire, for instance, hoping to draw him into one last feud. To avoid any such rancor, Stoner drags his ailing body through a dismal retirement dinner. He's too weak to teach, but meets with his doctoral students during the day and reads over their theses and dissertations at night.

The last ten pages of the book take place in his study, a little room that he knows will become his entire world. He forgives, and is forgiven, by Edith, who cares for him as he grows weaker. ("She has her child again, he thought, at last she has her child that she can care for.")

Grace appears and his mind drifts back to the era of their quiet communion. He can see the still, beautiful child she was. He hears her small laughter echo in the distance. "You were always there," he murmurs. But she can't go back there with him. The disappointment is too much for her to bear. She stares at her father "almost in disbelief," then turns away. It's the last time Stoner will see his daughter and he knows it.

His friend Gordon Finch appears and Stoner, his mind again unmoored within the flow of time, asks, "Where's Dave?" He means Dave Masters, "the defiant boy they had both loved" as young graduate students. But Finch is alarmed to have this ghost awakened, and unsettled by Stoner's physical deterioration. Like Grace, he turns away and quits the room.

This is how death often plays out. Survivors do not always look upon the dying with a misty benevolence and a determination to love them purely before the end. They are more often besieged by complex and harrowing feelings: fear, guilt, anger, betrayal. That's a start. Nobody wants to face what's happening.

*

Stoner is an exception. He has no wish to die. And yet, after bidding his farewells, there are moments when he looks forward to death impatiently, and others in which he covets solitude, knowing that the dying can be selfish: "They want their moments to themselves, like children."

He has one final relationship to reckon with: the one with himself. This process begins with a voice speaking to him. He has reached a point in his illness where he can't always recognize who is in the room with him, or make out what they're saying. He knows only that someone is talking about his life. Suddenly, "with the fierceness of a wounded animal" his mind pounces on the question of how others view his life.

"Dispassionately, reasonably, Stoner contemplated the failure that his life must appear to be." He has had two friends, one of whom suffered a premature and senseless death. He sought the "still connective passion" of marriage and it, too, died almost before it began. He desired and found love with Katherine, yet relinquished it. He became a teacher but was an indifferent one for most of his life. "He had dreamed of a kind of integrity, of a kind of purity that was entire; he had found compromise and the assaulting diversion of triviality. He had conceived wisdom, and at the end of the long years he had found ignorance. And what else? he thought. What else?"

Everyone harbors this merciless voice of judgment. It's the byproduct of a mind that measures worth using the math of the obituary, in which only the visibly heroic survives the final edit—life minus the inner life. In Stoner's case, this lacerating appraisal may also represent a protective impulse: it's easier to depart a failed life, after all.

But something fascinating happens after Stoner's done pummeling himself. He falls into a lengthy slumber and awakens with his strength returned. He lifts himself up in bed and feels sun and shade upon his face. He gazes at the "sheen upon the leaves of the huge elm tree" in his backyard. He smells the early summer air "crowded with the sweet odors of grass and leaf and flower" and breaths "the sweetness of the summer" into his lungs. A child of barren soil, Stoner has always been exquisitely attuned to the natural world. Here, roused from his moment of doubt, sensation swoops in to revive him.

He knows that he's close to death, but calmness envelopes him, as if he "has all the time in the world." He hears laughter and notices a trio of young couples cutting across his yard. "The girls were long-limbed and graceful in their light summer dresses, and the boys were looking at them with a joyous and bemused wonder. They walked lightly upon the grass, hardly touching it, leaving no trace of where they had been."

Stoner is suffused with an abrupt joy, which signals the arrival of grace within the perishing body: "He dimly recalled that he had been thinking of failure—as if it mattered. It seemed to him now that such thoughts were mean, unworthy of what his life had been."

*

He dimly recalled that he had been thinking of failure—as if it mattered.

Has there ever been a more forgiving sentence written in the English language, a more hopeful sentence? It represents the eternal wish: that the arrival of death will cleanse our souls of the petty judgment by which we dishonor the miracle of our inner lives.

As someone who struggles with that voice of petty judgment, someone who has dedicated his life, fitfully, to the transmission of love through the arrest of attention, someone who yearns openly for such a state of grace, I have been elated, always, to encounter this line. It's like the chunk of chocolate that used to drift to the bottom of the pints of ice cream I devoured on summer evenings, in the days before lactose lanced my aging gut.

But a strange thing happened the last time I arrived at this line: I broke down sobbing. I broke down sobbing because I thought of my mother and the long, agonizing manner of her death.

*

It makes no sense to describe that death, as *Stoner* attests, without telling something of the life that preceded it. Barbara Almond was born in 1938, and raised in the Bronx. Her parents were Jewish immigrants who lived in the tenements of the Lower East Side. They grew up during the Great Depression and because of what they saw in those years, they concluded that the bounty of the earth should be divided more or less equally among its inhabitants. This was a dangerous view to hold in the years after World War II, and my grandmother, who taught grade school in Harlem, was eventually hauled before the New York City Board of Education. This was all part of the work done by the House Committee on Un-American Activities. Rather than testify, my grandmother retired.

My mother never knew the full extent of her parents' political activities but, like little Grace Stoner, she absorbed the anxiety that flowed through their apartment, along with a pervasive sense of secrecy.

Both my grandparents were strivers, and my grandfather, in particular, pushed my mom to achieve. She wound up as one of five women in the Yale Medical School class of 1960, scattered among eighty-five men, one of whom was my father. During her residency, she gave birth to three children, all boys, in the space of two years. Amid all this, she protested for civil rights and later joined the anti-war movement.

During my childhood, she saw patients all day, then raced home and got dinner on the table and did most of the household cleaning. She was, by any objective measure, a powerful and accomplished woman, a respected therapist, a brilliant pianist, a loving matriarch.

But there were moments when the strain became unmistakable. Sometimes, as she drove around on errands, she would forget we were in the backseat and I could hear her drift into addled soliloquys, whispered enumerations of all that weighed upon her. Or I would catch sight of her staring into the distance, shaking her head, as if seeking to make peace with the burdens of her circumstance, or gathering herself for the next depredation.

She was bullied in our family, as I've noted, the unacknowledged victim of masculine privilege and the assumed healer of masculine doubt. (I believe I have just described every woman on earth.) She didn't have enough allies, really. It was all sons and patriarchs.

When my older brother graduated from medical school, my mom called her father to share the good news. "Well, pop," she said, "we've got three doctors in the family now."

Her father paused. Then he asked, in genuine puzzlement: "Oh yeah, who's the third?"

My mother had by this time had been a psychiatrist in private practice for twenty-five years and was training to become a psychoanalyst.

*

Many years later, on a vacation in the mountains, I went on a hike with my parents, during which my father, an intrepid trekker, pushed my mom to embrace certain challenges—a perilous river crossing, a steep, exposed trail—for which she didn't feel physically equipped. This led to a few long, tense, humiliating episodes. By which I mean that my mom was immobilized by terror, sometimes on her hands and knees. I should have defended her. I should have apologized. But I was afraid of my father's disapproval, and I saw in her struggle too much of my own weakness.

My mom made it through the hike but wound up in the ER with a racing heart. When we met the next day, she had recovered physically, but was uncharacteristically subdued. I assumed she was ashamed, though I can see now that I was ashamed. She glanced down for a moment then said, very quietly, "Stevie, I was the nigger of this family."

Why would my mother—who had marched into segregated restaurants with African-American students and demanded service—utter such an indefensible word?

She was struggling, I think, to convey how powerless she felt, the enormity of the hurt she'd experienced living within our family, nearly all of it invisible. The word was meant to startle and offend, in the same way Yoko Ono and John Lennon meant when they released "Woman Is the Nigger of the

World." Or maybe it would be more accurate to say that she was simply unburdening herself of her most closely guarded secret: the sorrow of her inner life.

*

I think of this episode, in part, because the last decade of my mother's life was conducted under the shadow of calamity and illness. On a family vacation, while walking to the store to buy ketchup for her grandkids, she was hit by a truck and suffered a broken pelvis and internal bleeding. The next summer, doctors found the first cancer.

Still later, between the second and third cancers, she fell on the path outside her office. This fall had a curious effect. It sent her tumbling back to the Bronx of her childhood. She kept asking where her mother was. She was certain I was her uncle. Sometimes she would wake to find herself lying in a strange white room with needles and tubes taped to her arms. "Stevie," she would whisper. "I've just had the most terrible dream."

By the end of it, my mother had endured half a dozen bouts with cancers and chemo, two surgeries, and radiation. All this "treatment" exacerbated a cognitive decline that dulled her fierce intellect, impaired her work, and, toward the end, robbed her of the great refuge of her life, which was reading.

During one of her deliriums, I sat by her bed and read her Dickens, her favorite author. I'd chosen *David Copperfield*, and I could see that my mother—who now struggled to recall her home address—knew the first chapter by heart. The novel begins, of course, with this immortal line: *Whether I shall turn out to be the hero of my own life, or whether that station will be held by anybody else, these pages must show.*

If only that were how it worked.

But it is we, the authors of our lives, who are charged with that obligation. We are the ones who must decide whether we led lives of meaning, whether, like Stoner, we came to know and accept ourselves at the end. And it is here that I must square up and face the truth I keep dancing around, which is that my mother was disgraced by the process of dying.

Having worked so hard to build a career, and seen her troubled sons into lives of stability, she yearned to reap what she had spent so long in sowing, to deepen her work as a psychoanalyst and writer, to indulge her young grandchildren, to live. Like many ambitious people, she experienced illness as a narcissistic injury. As cancer strafed her mind and body, she blamed herself for being weak. It was as if the journey toward death was another awful hike, designed, once again, to savage her dignity, to bring her to her knees.

*

I don't mean to suggest that her dying was without its idylls of grace. Like Stoner, she was exquisitely attuned to the beauty of the earth. My father took her on short hikes into the Stanford hills where she would pause to examine the wildflowers, to caress a petal between her fingertips, to drink in its color. She gazed at the oak trees and their skirts of black shadow. She closed her eyes and turned toward the sun. She listened to the birds.

She played piano when she had the strength, and the music of Mozart and Bach washed through the house, as it had throughout my childhood. Toward the end, when she could no longer play, she managed to attend a local concert of works by Schubert, her favorite composer. She had entered the concert hall so weak that my father had to support her. But as the music played, she felt flushed by a strange euphoria. "I don't know how to explain this," she wrote to me. "It was as if there was still beauty in the world."

She also retained her sense of humor to the very end. "There is some good news," she muttered, after her final surgery. "The doctors tell me there's not much left for them to take out." And still later she greeted an old friend who'd come to visit by rolling her eyes and doing a double take. "Well, I'll be damned," she said. "Not to get ahead of myself." Like all depressives, she understood the comic impulse as a form of self-forgiveness.

*

My mother felt so much about dying—terror, outrage, shame—that she could hardly acknowledge it was happening to her. Walking into her bedroom, one felt the smothering denial, that queasy code of silence that prevails when a group of people have agreed, tacitly and uneasily, to live within a frail dream. We couldn't talk about what was really happening. We couldn't say farewell.

And thus, my mother's anguish was redoubled by loneliness. For she alone was the person growing smaller, grayer, less responsive, bearing the mortal toll. As illness consumed her, she became more and more unsettled by our company. She turned inward, toward the self-doubt and anxiety that had been her most loyal companions.

There came a point, as in *Stoner*, where sickness took her hostage. She couldn't leave her room without the risk of collapse. We worried constantly that she would fall. One day, I came into her bedroom to check on her and saw that she had escaped her bed. The bathroom door was shut, and I could hear splashing.

She had managed to get herself into the bath somehow but lacked the strength to get herself out. It was left to my brother Dave and me to lift her from the tub and dry her skin and wipe away the trickles of blood from where she had tried to shave her legs. She was trembling violently the entire time, in tears, clutching at a towel, panicked at the thought that her sons would see her ravaged body. Her body looked beautiful. She looked like Eve.

I should admit here that I felt a special burden, in part because I was living across the country as my mother died, but also because I saw us as life-long allies: the family empaths, the left-handers, the readers. I had always known how vulnerable she was, beneath her indomitable energies, and I felt, in some secret part of myself, that it was my duty to make her happy, to dance the tango with her across the scuffed floors of our kitchen, to get her giggling when she was blue by imitating Harpo Marx.

For this reason, it was difficult to spend time with her at the end, because there was nothing I could do to quell her despair, to lure her back into the province of hope. William Stoner reached out to his loved ones at the end. But my mother had gone the other way. I couldn't reach her, and, feeling helpless, I fled.

Every child probably thinks this of his mother, that he's the special one, so I'll admit that this is just my version of the story. But much later, at one of those dreadful gatherings where the guest of honor is missing, a young woman who had tended to my mother in her final weeks took me aside. She told me that my mother had sat up at one point and looked around, suddenly alert. Then she had spoken a single word.

"Stevie?"

*

One of her last coherent conversations was with her sister Alice, with whom she had shared a bedroom, all those years ago in the Bronx. "So I didn't get an A-plus," my mother declared. "So what?" Then, in Bronxian bemusement, she blew a raspberry.

It was a kind of bewildered epitaph. But beneath the sly humor, I heard the scoff of judgment. My mother had, by then, survived years longer than the doctors who discovered her first cancer expected. Between bouts of chemo, she had written her critically acclaimed book about maternal ambivalence and continued to see patients and supervise training analysts. She flew east half a dozen times to visit her grandchildren.

She lived and died heroically by all accounts but the one that mattered: her own. Until the very end, she believed she was falling short. She lacked the strength to cook us meals, to come downstairs, to read stories to the kids, to drink her chocolate milkshakes. She was consumed by a sense of inadequacy, and her dying only affirmed that failure.

This is why *Stoner* haunts me. Because its final pages present a vision of death that is quietly triumphant. For all his shortcomings, William Stoner learns to exist in relation to himself. That languor creeps upon his limbs. He experiences that sudden sense of his own identity, and feels the power of it: *He was himself, and he knew what he had been.*

My mother deserved that. She deserved to die at peace with her inner life, to spend her final moments in the promised land of forgiveness.

*

In the closing paragraphs of *Stoner*, the dying man reaches out and grasps the book he wrote years ago. He knows the volume will be forgotten, that it served no use. But the question of its utility seems "almost trivial. He did not have the illusion that he would find himself there, in that fading print; and yet, he knew, a small part of him that he could not deny was there and would be there."

Stoner riffles his fingers through the book and feels a tingling, as if the pages are alive. Then his fingers loosen and the book tumbles from them and "into the silence of the room."

I can remember how I felt when I reached these words for the first time. I was sitting in that little carriage house in North Carolina, having read the book straight through. At some point, night had come and gone and wound a purple ribbon around the edge of the dawn. I was still dreaming that I was going to be a famous writer someday, revered and remembered.

I was so grateful to be alive! To have found such a wise and merciful book, to have become, in some mystical manner, a student of William Stoner. And at the very same instant,

I felt the poison of pure desolation, in the knowledge that I would never write such a novel, would never summon the attention necessary to transmit my love so purely.

It's twenty-five years later now and I feel the same way. I've published more books than I dared imagine and become a teacher and found a lovely wife and become a father to three fragile and ecstatic souls. I've made a life of deep connection and meaning.

And still, I live in terror of the possibility that I'll leave this world as my mother did, trembling, untouched by mercy, consumed by the novels unwritten, the relationships botched, the years squandered in egoism and distraction. That I'll have come all this way only to discover my inner life is as broken and cruel as the world around it.

That, my friends, is why I keep reading *Stoner*. Because every time I open the book Stoner is still perched at the front of the classroom, ready to bear my complaints, to sort me out. And the part of this story I love the most is that when I give myself over to the guy and let everything else drift away, when it's just him and me with one heart between us, he does something perfectly absurd: he laughs.

There I am, strangling the English language, dreading death, rehearsing my indictments, and William Stoner—who barely snickers during the course of his literary life—laughs so hard he can barely get the words out: "Is that you again, Almond? You're still thinking about failure? Okay, let's try this again."

Acknowledgments

With undying gratitude to:

Erin Almond for her wise and generous feedback, and her partnership in the hard work of love.

My parents for doing that same work in raising me and my brothers.

William Giraldi for his singular mind and faithful counsel.

My own extended family of friends (Cheryl Strayed, Tom DeMarchi, Clay Martin, David Blair, Camille Dungy, Victor Cruz, Zach Leber, Pat Flood, Sean Thomas, Keith Morris, Paul Salopek) for hearing me out.

Curtis Smith for suggesting I write this book, and the folks at Ig for agreeing to publish it.

John Williams for giving the world *Stoner*.

All the members of the Cult of *Stoner*.

My three children for being exactly who they are.